TWENTY-FIRST CENTURY
SUBMARINES

UNDERSEA VESSELS OF TODAY'S NAVIES

TWENTY-FIRST CENTURY
SUBMARINES

UNDERSEA VESSELS OF TODAY'S NAVIES

Steve Crawford

Grange
BOOKS

This edition published in 2003 by Grange Books
Grange Books plc
The Grange
1-6 Kingsnorth Estate
Hoo
Near Rochester
Kent
ME3 9ND
UK
www.grangebooks.co.uk

ISBN 1-84013-550-6

Editorial and design:
The Brown Reference Group plc
8 Chapel Place
Rivington Street
London
EC2A 3DQ
UK

Printed in China

Editors: James Murphy, Helen Knox
Picture Researchers: Andrew Webb, Susannah Jayes
Designer: Seth Grimbly
Production Director: Alastair Gourlay

PICTURE CREDITS
Bae Systems: 71.
Chinese Defence Today (www.sinodefence.com): 9, 10.
Electric Boat: 92.
Kockums: 65, 66, 67.
MPL: 11, 17, 38.
Nordseewerke GmbH: 35.
PA Photos: 24.
Private Collection: 6, 7, 8, 12, 13, 14, 15, 16, 18, 19, 20,
21, 22, 24, 25, 26, 27, 28, 29, 30, 31, 32, 33, 34, 36, 37,
39, 40, 41, 42, 44, 46, 47, 48, 49, 51, 52, 53, 54, 55, 56,
58, 59, 60, 61, 62, 63, 64, 68, 69, 70, 72, 73, 74, 75, 78,
79, 84, 85, 86, 87, 90, 91, 94, 95.
TRH: 23, 43, 45, 50, 57, 76, 77.
Rex: 42.
US DoD: 80, 81, 82, 83, 88, 89, 93.

CONTENTS

SAN JUAN

The *San Juan* is one of two Santa Cruz class attack submarines in service with the Argentine Navy. The TR1700 design, upon which the Santa Cruz class is based, comes from the Thyssen Nordseewerke shipbuilders. The original contract was for six boats to be delivered to Argentina. The first two were delivered complete and the subsequent vessels were to have materials supplied so that they could be built indigenously in Argentina's dockyards, thereby creating valuable jobs in an economy that needs such boosts desperately. However, all has not gone according to plan for the *Armada Argentina*. Two of the additional boats being built in Argentina, it is almost certain, will not be completed. Furthermore, the equipment procured for the fifth and sixth units of the class is being used for spares since Argentina cannot afford to buy spares direct from the contractor, Thyssen Nordseewerke. Without doubt, the fragile nature of Argentina's economic situation coupled with the internal political turmoil, has directly led to the drastic cutbacks being seen in its armed forces. With the future still looking uncertain for the recovery of Argentina's precarious circumstance, the two Santa Cruz submarines could well be the only attack submarines available to the Argentine Navy for some time to come, and may well serve long beyond their original service lives.

SPECIFICATIONS

Builder:	*Thyssen Nordseewerke*
Class:	*Santa Cruz (TR1700)*
Number:	*S-42*
Mission:	*attack submarine*
Length:	*65.9m (217ft)*
Beam:	*7.3m (24ft)*
Displacement:	*2264 tonnes (2300 tons)*
Speed:	*25 knots*
Operating Depth:	*250m (825ft)*
Maximum Depth:	*300m (990ft)*
Crew:	*50*
Nuclear Weapons:	*none*
Conventional Weapons:	*533mm (21in) torpedo, mines*
Sonar:	*Krupp-Atlas CSU-83*
Navigation:	*unknown*
Powerplant:	*diesel-electric, 8000 shp*
Date Commissioned:	*1985*

HMAS WALLER

The Royal Australian Navy's Collins class submarine is a long-range, multi-purpose attack submarine, and has been in service, despite some teething troubles, since 1999. The project is the most ambitious defence project ever undertaken in Australia, which is perhaps why there has been some difficulty in getting the boats into full operational service. It is capable of both short-duration coastal missions in littoral (shallow water) environments, and long-duration open-sea defensive and offensive operations. This makes the Collins class a very flexible weapons platform, and well suited to the demands of modern conflict and international peacekeeping or peace-enforcement. The Collins class has a patrol endurance of more than two months, and can spend most of this time submerged. However, as with all diesel-electric submarines, it needs some time on the surface to discharge exhaust fumes whilst recharging its batteries. With a displacement of over 3000 tonnes (3048 tons), the Collins class boats are some of the largest conventionally powered submarines in the world, on a similar scale to the Russian Kilo class. The project has not been cheap to implement, however, nor has it been without criticism, as the number of Collins class submarines to enter into Australian service totals six at present, at an estimated cost of over five billion Australian dollars (three billion US dollars).

SPECIFICATIONS

Builder:	*Kockums ASC*
Class:	*Collins*
Number:	*75*
Mission:	*attack submarine*
Length:	*78m (257ft)*
Beam:	*8m (26ft)*
Displacement:	*3350 tonnes (3403 tons)*
Speed:	*20 knots*
Operating Depth:	*250m (825ft)*
Maximum Depth:	*300m (990ft)*
Crew:	*42*
Nuclear Weapons:	*none*
Conventional Weapons:	*533mm (21in) torpedo, Harpoon*
Sonar:	*Thomson Sintra Scylla sonar suite*
Navigation:	*Kelvin Hughes Type 1007*
Powerplant:	*diesel-electric, 5000 shp*
Date Commissioned:	*1999*

TUPI

The Brazilian Navy's submarine force is based at Base Almirante Castro e Silva, Mocangue Island, just across the bay to the east of Rio de Janeiro. The force operates four Tupi class vessels and plans to have two Improved Tupi or Tikuna class submarines in service by the year 2005. The first-of-class submarine, *Tupi* (S30), was designed and built in Kiel, Germany, by Howaldtswerke Deutsche Werft (HDW) and commissioned into the Brazilian Navy in 1989. As is often the case with military foreign contract sales, the following vessels were built indigenously to the specification of the original. The Arsenal de Marinha naval shipyard in Rio de Janeiro has constructed three subsequent submarines over an extended period of 10 years, with the *Tamoio* commissioned in 1994, the *Timbira* commissioned in 1996 and the *Tapajo* commissioned in 1999. The *Tikuna*, an Improved Tupi class submarine, is under construction and is scheduled to commission in 2004, followed by the *Tapuia* in 2005. The submarine is equipped with quite sophisticated electronics, including two Mod 76 periscopes supplied by Kollmorgen, the Calypso III I-band navigation radar from Thales, and the submarine's hull-mounted sonar is the CSU-83/1 from STN Atlas Electronik. It is armed with eight torpedo tubes from which it can launch 533mm (21in) torpedoes, or mines.

SPECIFICATIONS

Builder:	Arsenal de Marinha
Class:	Tupi (Type 209/1400)
Number:	S-30
Mission:	attack submarine
Length:	61m (201ft)
Beam:	6.2m (20ft)
Displacement:	1440 tonnes (1463 tons)
Speed:	24 knots
Operating Depth:	270m (891ft)
Maximum Depth:	350m (1155ft)
Crew:	30
Nuclear Weapons:	none
Conventional Weapons:	533mm (21in) torpedo, mines
Sonar:	STN Atlas Electronik CSU-83/1
Navigation:	Thales Calypso
Powerplant:	diesel-electric, 2400 shp
Date Commissioned:	1989

CHANGZHENG 5

The Type 091, also known as the Han class, is China's first nuclear submarine. The first ship, number 401, was completed in 1974 but did not become fully operational until the 1980s due to the unreliability of its nuclear power plant and the lack of a suitable torpedo weapons system. It is believed that the French were heavily involved in aiding the upgrading of the Type 091, including help with a modified nuclear reactor with a much-reduced acoustic signature, the addition of a French-designed intercept sonar set, and the replacement of the original Soviet ESM equipment with an unknown French design. From the third ship (403) the submarine was lengthened by 8m (26ft) to be fitted with the YJ-82 anti-ship missile. All six ships are reportedly based at Jianggezhuang (Qingdao) Navy Base in the People's Liberation Army Navy (PLAN) North Sea Fleet, though other reports claimed that some of these ships may be temporarily assigned to the South Sea Fleet. The first two ships (401, 402) were refitted in the late 1980s, and back in service in the mid-1990s. Numbers 403 and 404 started mid-life refits in 1998 and were back in service in 2000. As with a great deal of Chinese equipment, unanswered questions hang over the Type 091, and it remains to be seen whether the Han class is a truly worthy attack submarine, able to stand against modern US boats.

SPECIFICATIONS

Builder:	Huludao Shipyard
Class:	Han (Type 091)
Number:	404
Mission:	attack submarine
Length:	98m (324ft)
Beam:	10m (33ft)
Displacement:	5500 tonnes (5588 tons)
Speed:	25 knots
Operating Depth:	unknown
Maximum Depth:	unknown
Crew:	75
Nuclear Weapons:	none
Conventional Weapons:	533mm (21in) torpedo, YJ-82
Sonar:	Trout Cheek sonar suite
Navigation:	Snoop Tray
Powerplant:	nuclear reactor, shp unknown
Date Commissioned:	1990

CHANGZHENG 6

The Type 092, also known as the Xia class, is China's first and only ballistic missile nuclear submarine (SSBN). It is derived from the Type 091 Han class, with the hull lengthened to accommodate the 12 missile tubes. The first ship, *Changzheng 6*, was launched in 1981 and became operational in 1983, though the JL-1 missile did not conduct a successful test launch until 1988 due to problems with its fire-control system. A second ship was reportedly constructed, but was later lost in an accident in 1985. The first test launch of the JL-1 submarine-launched ballistic missile (SLBM) took place in 1984. The first launch from a Type 092 was in 1985 but was unsuccessful, delaying the vessel's entrance into operational service. It was not until 1988 that a satisfactory launch took place. Currently the People's Liberation Army Navy (PLAN) has only one boat, *Changzheng 6*, which is deployed with the North Sea Fleet. The submarine has recently undergone an extensive refit with the upgrades reportedly including replacement of the original JL-1 missile with the improved JL-1A, which has an extended range of 4000km (2500 miles). Operations have been limited and the Type 092 has never sailed beyond Chinese regional waters. Despite a potential for operations in the Pacific Ocean, capabilities would be very limited against modern Western or Russian ASW capabilities.

SPECIFICATIONS

Builder:	Huludao Shipyard
Class:	Xia (Type 092)
Number:	406
Mission:	ballistic missile submarine
Length:	120m (396ft)
Beam:	10m (33ft)
Displacement:	6500 tonnes (6604 tons)
Speed:	22 knots
Operating Depth:	unknown
Maximum Depth:	unknown
Crew:	140
Nuclear Weapons:	12 x Ju Lang-1A SLBMs
Conventional Weapons:	533mm (21in) torpedo, mines
Sonar:	unknown
Navigation:	Snoop Tray
Powerplant:	nuclear reactor
Date Commissioned:	1986

YUANZHANG 67

China ordered two Kilo class diesel-electric submarines from Russia in 1996, and they were delivered in 1998. These two boats are the standard export version Kilo, Type 877EKM. China also ordered another two Improved Kilo, Type 636 version of the Kilo class submarines, which were delivered in 2000. The Kilo class is undoubtedly the most capable submarine in service with the People's Liberation Army Navy (PLAN). Once their crews are fully trained, these new diesel submarines will provide a substantial improvement in China's attack submarine capability. They will enhance China's capability to interdict commercial or naval shipping, and hence deny sea control to potentially hostile forces operating in China's coastal areas. Currently all four Kilo vessels are deployed as part of the East Sea Fleet and ought to remain as one of China's most important naval assets well into the twenty-first century. Reportedly, however, the first two Kilo submarines have engaged in only limited sea operations due to engine problems. Latest reports appear to confirm that China has recently ordered another eight Type 636 Improved Kilo class submarines from Russia, for a total of 12 boats in service by 2005. These submarines may be fitted with an Air Independent Propulsion (AIP) system and carry the Klub submerged-launch anti-ship missiles.

SPECIFICATIONS

Builder:	Huludao Shipyard
Class:	Kilo
Number:	367
Mission:	attack submarine
Length:	73m (241ft)
Beam:	9.9m (33ft)
Displacement:	3000 tons (3048 tons)
Speed:	20 knots
Operating Depth:	300m (990ft)
Maximum Depth:	400m (1320ft)
Crew:	52
Nuclear Weapons:	none
Conventional Weapons:	533mm (21in) torpedo, Klub
Sonar:	MGK-400M
Navigation:	unknown
Powerplant:	diesel-electric, 6000 shp
Date Commissioned:	1991

HMS KRONBORG

The original HMS *Nacken* was launched in 1978 as the lead submarine in the Nacken class for the Swedish Navy, a class consisting of three submarines. However, HMS *Nacken* has recently been extensively modernized, and was the test platform for the Air Independent Propulsion (AIP) system built into the new Gotland class and the refitted Sodermanland class. On the strength of its performance in these trials, and the fact that it would remain fitted with the AIP system, it was a very attractive prospect for purchase. Thus the Danish Navy stepped in with a bid to buy it, and in 2001 the *Nacken* was commissioned into service with the Danish Navy and renamed HMS *Kronborg*. The purchase of this vessel marked a significant upgrading of the Danish Navy's war-fighting capabilities. Its existing fleet of Tumleren class boats lacked the technology of the Nacken, and the Danish Navy found itself less able to cooperate with its allies. With the introduction of HMS *Kronborg*, however, the technology gap between the Danish Navy and her Scandinavian neighbours has now been plugged until the pan-Scandinavian Viking project comes into service. In addition to the improvement in capability, HMS *Kronborg* provides Danish crews with vital experience of a modern vessel, which will be invaluable when the next-generation boats enter Danish service.

SPECIFICATIONS

Builder:	*Kockums*
Class:	*Kronborg*
Number:	*S-325*
Mission:	*attack submarine*
Length:	*57.9m (191ft)*
Beam:	*5.7m (19ft)*
Displacement:	*1218 tonnes (1237 tons)*
Speed:	*20 knots*
Operating Depth:	*250m (825ft)*
Maximum Depth:	*350m (1155ft)*
Crew:	*19*
Nuclear Weapons:	*none*
Conventional Weapons:	*533mm (21in) torpedo, mines*
Sonar:	*Atlas Electronik CSU-83 sonar*
Navigation:	*Terna radar*
Powerplant:	*diesel-electric AIP, 1500 shp*
Date Commissioned:	*2001*

HMS SÆLEN

The three submarines of the Tumleren class are of the German Type 207 design. In 1964–66 they were built at the Rheinstahl-Nordseewerke in Germany for the Norwegian Navy as part of the 15 units of the Kobben class. In 1989–91 three units of the Kobben class were purchased and taken over by the Royal Danish Navy from Norway. Following an extensive refit they were renamed *HMS Tumleren*, *HMS Sælen* and *HMS Springeren* and replaced the four boats of the older Danish-designed and built Delfinen class. The Danish submarines are equipped and trained for an emphasis on littoral operations. This reflects the geography of Denmark and its historical and strategic position of controlling the entrance to the Baltic Sea. Since the birth of the Danish submarine force in 1909, the ability to operate in shallow and confined waters has been of prime importance. In addition, the more traditional open-water operations in the North Atlantic region are exercised routinely by participation in NATO's Standing Naval Force Atlantic. Following the end of the Cold War and NATO's new strategic concept, the tasks of the Danish armed forces have been redirected towards international operations such as peacekeeping and peace-enforcement. Such operations will typically require enhanced littoral capabilities encompassing all the different kinds of submarine warfare.

SPECIFICATIONS

Builder:	*Howaldtswerke-Deutsche Werft*
Class:	*Tumleren*
Number:	*S-323*
Mission:	*coastal patrol*
Length:	*46.6m (154ft)*
Beam:	*4.6m (15ft)*
Displacement:	*524 tonnes (532 tons)*
Speed:	*17 knots*
Operating Depth:	*200m (660ft)*
Maximum Depth:	*270m (891ft)*
Crew:	*18*
Nuclear Weapons:	*none*
Conventional Weapons:	*533mm (21in) torpedo, mines*
Sonar:	*PSU-83*
Navigation:	*unknown*
Powerplant:	*diesel-electric, 1700 shp*
Date Commissioned:	*1990*

AMÉTHYSTE

The French Navy's Améthyste class attack submarine is a follow-on development from the successful Rubis class SSN. It has been designed for littoral anti-submarine operations, but like most modern submarines can perform a varied number of jobs with efficiency, including anti-shipping, reconnaissance and power-projection missions. The Améthyste class incorporates many improvements on the original Rubis design to make it a more capable machine. These include a slightly longer hull to incorporate a quieter propulsion system, and a much improved electronics suite. In addition to the 533mm (21in) torpedoes, the Améthyste class can launch the ship-killing Exocet missile. The missile is guided by target range and bearing data from the submarine's tactical data system and weapons control system, which is downloaded into the Exocet's onboard computer. The missile approaches the target area in a sea-skimming fashion using inertial navigation to avoid detection, and then uses active radar homing as it nears the target. The missile approaches the target at speeds of over Mach 0.9 (1170 km/h) and the range is 50km (31.25 miles). The Exocet is armed with a 165kg (363lb) high-explosive shaped charge and is utterly deadly. Exocet missiles sank the British ships HMS *Sheffield* and *Atlantic Conveyor* during the 1982 Falklands War.

SPECIFICATIONS

Builder:	DCN International
Class:	Améthyste
Number:	S-605
Mission:	attack submarine
Length:	73.6m (241ft)
Beam:	7.6m (25ft)
Displacement:	2730 tonnes (2774 tons)
Speed:	25 knots
Operating Depth:	200m (660ft)
Maximum Depth:	300m (990ft)
Crew:	70
Nuclear Weapons:	none
Conventional Weapons:	533mm (21in) torpedo, Exocet
Sonar:	Thomson Sintra DMUX 20
Navigation:	Thomson-CSF DRUA 33
Powerplant:	nuclear reactor, 9500 shp
Date Commissioned:	1992

EMERAUDE

The French Navy has modified four of its older Rubis class attack submarines, to bring them up to a similar standard to the more modern Améthyste class SSNs. The resulting hybrid class is known as the Rubis-Améthyste. The French Navy operates its Rubis-Améthyste class submarines from the naval base in Toulon. The first batch of Rubis class submarines was initially equipped for an anti-surface role, but since becoming the Rubis-Améthyste class they have been re-equipped to the same standard as the later Améthyste submarines, giving them the capability to perform both anti-surface and anti-submarine warfare missions. This has been achieved by the addition of two extra torpedo tubes, and improved sonar, radar and navigation systems. The submarine has the capacity to carry 14 missiles and torpedoes in a mixed load. The four 533mm (21in) torpedo tubes are equipped with a pneumatic ram system for discharging torpedoes from the tubes. The Rubis-Améthyste is armed with two types of torpedo. One is the ECAN L5 Mod 3 torpedo. This is equipped with active and passive homing and has a range of 9.5km (6 miles). The torpedo has a speed of 35 knots and delivers a 150kg (330lb) warhead to a depth of 550m (1815ft). The ECAN F17 Mod 2 torpedo is a wire-guided torpedo with a range of over 20km (12.5 miles) and a depth of up to 600m (1980ft).

SPECIFICATIONS

Builder:	DCN International
Class:	Rubis-Améthyste
Number:	S-604
Mission:	attack submarine
Length:	72.1m (236ft)
Beam:	7.6m (25ft)
Displacement:	2670 tonnes (2712 tons)
Speed:	25 knots
Operating Depth:	250m (825ft)
Maximum Depth:	300m (990ft)
Crew:	70
Nuclear Weapons:	none
Conventional Weapons:	533mm (21in) torpedo, Exocet
Sonar:	Thomson Sintra DMUX 20
Navigation:	Thomson-CSF DRUA 33
Powerplant:	nuclear reactor, 9500 shp
Date Commissioned:	1988 (recommissioned 1996)

L'INDOMPTABLE

The French Navy's *L'Indomptable* vessel has been retained in service despite being slated for decommissioning in the 1990s, and is expected to remain so until 2004. This vessel carries a compliment of 130 men, of whom 15 are officers. Like most ballistic missile submarines (SSBNs) the crew is divided into two, *rouge* (red) and *bleu* (blue), who keep a continual 24-hour watch. This means that the vessel can react to emergency order immediately, rather than having to prepare. The ability to carry out emergency orders immediately is a key part of strategic deterrence, since any potential aggressor must be aware that attack will be met with an immediate response. The French Navy's SSBNs have not seen as much active service as the US or British fleets, but they continue to patrol the world's oceans protecting France's interests. Whereas the British SSBN submarine fleet takes response orders and targeting parameters from the US, the French president retains the sole right to give the order to launch France's nuclear weapons. In reality, however, France is unlikely to act alone in any given international crisis where the threat of nuclear force is present. The M4 submarine-launched ballistic missile (SLBM) that is carried by the L'Inflexible class is capable of hitting six different targets up to 4000km (2500 miles) away.

SPECIFICATIONS

Builder:	DCN International
Class:	L'Inflexible
Number:	S-613
Mission:	ballistic missile submarine
Length:	128m (420ft)
Beam:	10.5m (35ft)
Displacement:	9000 tonnes (9144 tons)
Speed:	25 knots
Operating Depth:	280m (924ft)
Maximum Depth:	350m (1155ft)
Crew:	130
Nuclear Weapons:	16 x M4 SLBM
Conventional Weapons:	533mm (21in) torpedo, Exocet
Sonar:	Thomson Sintra DSUX 21
Navigation:	Thomson-CSF DRUA 33
Powerplant:	nuclear reactor, 16,000 shp
Date Commissioned:	1976 (recommissioned 1989)

L'INFLEXIBLE

The L'inflexible class ballistic missile submarines were the result of a modernizing of the ageing Le Redoubtable class SSBNs launched in the early 1970s. The French have traditionally developed their own nuclear technology, which meant that their sea-based nuclear deterrence was lagging far behind the US and US-aided British SSBNs. When the original Le Redoubtable class was launched it was already behind the times, and thus a modernization plan brought the class up to L'Inflexible standards. When the vessel bearing the name *Le Redoubtable* was decommissioned in 1991, all remaining boats became known as L'Inflexible class, irrespective of their original pre-overhaul configuration. This vessel is part of France's Strategic Oceanic Force (FOST), but it is due to retire from active duty in the next few years as the Le Triomphant class begins to enter service. Delays with the remaining Le Triomphant class vessels means that the L'Inflexible class boats will stay in service longer than the original 2003 retirement date. The last remaining vessel of the original L'Inflexible class has been recently retro-fitted with the M45 SLBM to reflect the fact that it will be in service longer than expected. Though no match for the most modern SSBNs around the world, they are still capable vessels and maintain France's nuclear deterrence.

SPECIFICATIONS

Builder:	DCN International
Class:	L'Inflexible
Number:	S-615
Mission:	ballistic missile submarine
Length:	128m (420ft)
Beam:	10.5m (35ft)
Displacement:	9000 tonnes (9144 tons)
Speed:	25 knots
Operating Depth:	280m (924ft)
Maximum Depth:	350m (1155ft)
Crew:	130
Nuclear Weapons:	16 x M45 SLBM
Conventional Weapons:	533mm (21in) torpedo, Exocet
Sonar:	Thomson Sintra DSUX 21
Navigation:	Thomson-CSF DRUA 33
Powerplant:	nuclear reactor, 16,000 shp
Date Commissioned:	1985

LE TÉMÉRAIRE

The new Le Triomphant class of ballistic missile submarine is an integral part of France's Strategic Oceanic Force (FOST). Much like the United Kingdom, French strategic doctrine demands that at least one SSBN be on patrol at any given time, able to launch a retaliatory second-strike in the event of an attack on France itself or any of her NATO allies. Though the world is a very different place since the collapse of communism in Russia, France still sees a necessity to develop and maintain an SSBN force, as well as keeping a nuclear bombing capability. The modern Le Triomphant class takes advantage of many developments in computer technology and materials advances to keep it ahead of its predecessor, the L'Inflexible class SSBN which entered service in the 1980s. It boasts a sophisticated sensor array that gives a very extensive detection range, and has a modern steel structure composed of US equivalent HY130 steel. This gives the class the ability to dive much deeper than its predecessor, thus making it more flexible and stealthy. Le Téméraire is the second vessel in a batch of four Le Triomphant class submarines to be launched, and by 2008 all four should be in service. Under the SNLE-NG (Sous-Marins Nucléaires Lanceurs Engins-Nouvelle Génération) programme, each Le Triomphant SSBN costs 5.5 billion Euros.

SPECIFICATIONS

Builder:	DCN International
Class:	Le Triomphant
Number:	S-617
Mission:	ballistic missile submarine
Length:	138m (452ft)
Beam:	12.5m (41ft)
Displacement:	14,120 tonnes (14,345 tons)
Speed:	25 knots
Operating Depth:	300m (990ft)
Maximum Depth:	400m (1320ft)
Crew:	110
Nuclear Weapons:	16 x M45 ballistic missiles
Conventional Weapons:	533mm (21in) torpedo, Exocet
Sonar:	DMUX 80 sonar suite
Navigation:	Racal 1229 DRBN 34A
Powerplant:	nuclear reactor, 41,000 shp
Date Commissioned:	1997

LE TRIOMPHANT

The French Navy's Le Triomphant class ballistic missile submarine is the replacement for the L'Inflexible M4 class SSBNs. The submarine was designed and built at DCN's (Direction des Constructions et Armes Navales) Cherbourg shipyard, and the first-of-class submarine was launched in July 1993 and entered service in 1997. There are to be four submarines in total in this class. The *Le Triomphant* carries 16 vertically launched M45 ballistic missiles with a warhead of six multiple re-entry vehicles (MRVs). Each MRV has the explosive power equivalent to 147,638 tons (150,000 tons) of TNT, making it 10 times more powerful than the A-bomb dropped on Hiroshima. The missile has a range of 6000km (3750 miles). A new enhanced M51 ballistic missile is due to enter service in 2008, and this will carry a warhead with 12 multiple independently targetable re-entry vehicles (MIRVs), and have an increased range of 8000km (5000 miles). Aside from its ballistic missiles, *Le Triomphant* carries the Exocet surface-to-surface anti-shipping missile, as well as a variety of torpedoes fired from its four 533mm (21in) torpedo tubes. France has invested large sums of money in modernizing and maintaining its strategic nuclear deterrence, and in *Le Triomphant* it has a vessel to take their nuclear capability into the twenty-first century.

SPECIFICATIONS

Builder:	DCN International
Class:	Le Triomphant
Number:	S-616
Mission:	ballistic missile submarine
Length:	138m (452ft)
Beam:	12.5m (41ft)
Displacement:	14,120 tonnes (14,345 tons)
Speed:	25+ knots
Operating Depth:	300m (990ft)
Maximum Depth:	400m (1320ft)
Crew:	110
Nuclear Weapons:	16 x M45 ballistic missiles
Conventional Weapons:	533mm (21in) torpedo, Exocet
Sonar:	DMUX 80 sonar suite
Navigation:	Racal 1229 DRBN 34A
Powerplant:	nuclear reactor, 41,000 shp
Date Commissioned:	1997

U18

The original Type 206 class attack submarines in the German Navy were commissioned between 1973 and 1975. By the end of the 1980s, a major programme of modifications upgraded 12 boats to the Type 206A class. This modernization was geared chiefly towards the introduction of an integrated computer-based combat and sonar system, and was completed in 1992. The Type 206A benefits from excellent manoeuvrability and depth-keeping capabilities, which enables it to operate submerged in water depths of just 18m (60ft). This is a great advantage in littoral operations where the seafloor often hinders larger submarines. Due to its small size, the Type 206A is quite an elusive target, both in terms of initial detection, and then tracking once found. The complement of 25 consists of 6 officers, 6 chief petty officers and 13 petty officers. The weapons control system is, among other features, capable of tracking several targets fully automatically and can handle a maximum of three wire-guided torpedoes simultaneously. When approaching the targets, the torpedoes will gain contact and lock their homing heads onto the target, but do not attack unless ordered to do so by the operator of the control system. Fitted with eight sophisticated torpedo tubes for use against surface and sub-surface vessels, the 206A has considerable firepower for its relatively diminutive size.

SPECIFICATIONS

Builder:	Howaldtswerke-Deutsche Werft
Class:	Type 206A
Number:	S-197
Mission:	attack submarine
Length:	48.6m (159ft)
Beam:	4.7m (15ft)
Displacement:	520 tonnes (528 tons)
Speed:	17 knots
Operating Depth:	180m (594ft)
Maximum Depth:	300m (990ft)
Crew:	25
Nuclear Weapons:	none
Conventional Weapons:	533mm (21in) torpedo, mines
Sonar:	Thomson Sintra DUUX 2
Navigation:	Thomson CSF Calypso II
Powerplant:	diesel-electric, 2300 shp
Date Commissioned:	1975

U31

The Type 212A class attack submarine is the latest in a long and illustrious line of German diesel-electric submarines from the HDW shipyard. The German ship-building industry is the largest exporter of submarines in the world, and the Type 212A has already been ordered by a number of different countries including Italy and Norway. The new Type 212A was designed for the German Navy, amongst others, with the faults of the Type 206 class vessels in mind, and the improvements in the new class attempt to address these. The modifications include a greater long-range reconnaissance and detection capability, as well as the introduction of a satellite communications system for a fast and secure means of exchanging information. Other modifications include a further improvement on the stealthiness of the submarine, faster and longer-range torpedoes, a high degree of automation, an improvement of living conditions onboard, and an improved environmental protection system. The most important technology to be included in the new class, however, is the Air Independent Propulsion (AIP) system. In this system, oxygen and hydrogen are combined in a catalytic way to release electrical energy (to power the vessel) and the waste products. This remarkable technology makes the Type 212A class exceptionally quiet, robust and thus more deadly.

SPECIFICATIONS

Builder:	Howaldtswerke-Deutsche Werft
Class:	Type 212A
Number:	S-181
Mission:	attack submarine
Length:	56m (185ft)
Beam:	7m (23ft)
Displacement:	1830 tonnes (1828 tons)
Speed:	20 knots
Operating Depth:	300m (990ft)
Maximum Depth:	400m (1320ft)
Crew:	27
Nuclear Weapons:	none
Conventional Weapons:	533mm (21in) torpedo, mines
Sonar:	DBQS-40 sonar suite
Navigation:	Kelvin Hughes Type 1007
Powerplant:	diesel-electric AIP, 4243 shp
Date Commissioned:	2003

PONTOS

The Glavkos class patrol/attack submarine is essentially a Greek version of the popular German-built Type 209 class. The Hellenic Navy was the first in the world to order this class of submarine, and the first vessel entered service in 1971. There are eight individual boats, in two variations in service with the Hellenic Navy. The first four boats of the class are Type 1100 and the last four are Type 1200, of which the *Pontos* is one. Despite the different designations, they are considered to be the same class. The Glavkos class is a relatively simple design, and is only moderately automated, making it somewhat outdated in the modern era. The Greek Government has sought to remedy this technological shortcoming by ordering the new Type 214 submarine from the German HDW shipbuilding company. The first four boats of the class have been overhauled in the last few years, giving them the capability to launch the Sub Harpoon anti-shipping missile. This has greatly increased their war-fighting ability. In addition to the Sub Harpoon surface-to-surface missile, the Glavkos class is equipped with eight torpedo tubes capable of firing 533m (21in) torpedoes. The Glavkos class is due to remain in service until the Hellenic Navy has completed its procurement of the enhanced Type 214 class submarines, also from the same German shipbuilders.

SPECIFICATIONS

Builder:	*Howaldtswerke-Deutsche Werft*
Class:	*Glavkos (Type 209/1200)*
Number:	*S-119*
Mission:	*patrol/attack submarine*
Length:	*55.9m (184ft)*
Beam:	*6.3m (21ft)*
Displacement:	*1285 tonnes (1306 tons)*
Speed:	*22 knots*
Operating Depth:	*300m (990ft)*
Maximum Depth:	*400m (1325ft)*
Crew:	*31*
Nuclear Weapons:	*none*
Conventional Weapons:	*533mm (21in) torpedo, Harpoon*
Sonar:	*Krupp 3-4 active/passive sonar*
Navigation:	*Calypso II radar*
Powerplant:	*diesel-electric, 5000 shp*
Date Commissioned:	*1980*

INS SHANKUL

After several years of discussion with Howaldtswerke-Deutsche Werft (HDW), the Indian Navy came to an agreement in December 1981 to purchase a number of the popular Type 209/1500 attack submarines for its fleet. The agreement clarified that the building in West Germany of two HDW 209 class vessels would be followed by a supply of packages for building two more at Mazagon Dockyards Ltd. In addition, HDW agreed to supply training to various groups of specialists for the design and construction of the last two submarines in the batch. The first two submarines sailed for India in February 1987, having been commissioned into Indian service the year before. In 1984 it was announced that two more submarines would be built at the Mazagon Dockyards Ltd (MDL) in Mumbai, but this was overtaken by events during the Kashmiri insurgency of 1987–88 and the agreement with HDW was terminated at just four submarines, rather than the original six. This was reconsidered in 1992 and again in 1997, but no orders have yet been placed. The Shishumar class began an extensive refit during 2000, which is thought to include improvements to the electronics suite, plus other minor improvements. The class can expect to be in service until the next decade of the twenty-first century, depending on certain economic and political factors.

SPECIFICATIONS

Builder:	Mazagon Dockyards Ltd/HDW
Class:	Shishumar (Type 209/1500)
Number:	S-47
Mission:	attack submarine
Length:	64.4m (213ft)
Beam:	6.5m (22ft)
Displacement:	1850 tonnes (1880 tons)
Speed:	22 knots
Operating Depth:	260m (863ft)
Maximum Depth:	350m (1155ft)
Crew:	40
Nuclear Weapons:	none
Conventional Weapons:	533mm (21in) torpedo, mines
Sonar:	Electronik CSU-83 sonar suite
Navigation:	Thomson-CSF Calypso
Powerplant:	diesel-electric, 4600 shp
Date Commissioned:	1994

INS SINDHUVIJAY

A total of 10 diesel-powered Kilo project 877EKM submarines, known in India as the Sindhugosh class, have been built under a contract between Russian shipbuilder Rosvooruzhenie and the Indian Defence Ministry. Kilo class submarines have been nicknamed "Black Hole" by NATO for their silent operation whilst on operations. In January 1997 two Improved Kilo class boats, also known as Kilo Type 636, were ordered by the Indian Navy and the first, INS *Sindhurakshak*, was commissioned in December 1997 at St Petersburg, Russia. This submarine was a spare Type 877EKM hull built for the Russian Navy, but was never purchased. The second, INS *Sindhushastra*, was commissioned in July 2000. The remaining Sindhugosh class vessels are the standard export versions of the 877EKM Kilo. The Sindhugosh class is fitted with six 533mm (21in) torpedo tubes, carrying 18 heavyweight torpedoes (6 in the tubes and 12 on the racks). It uses an automatic rapid loader which is remotely controlled from the main control panel or by the controls in the launch station. Two of the tubes can fire wire-guided torpedoes, whilst the other four have automatic reloading. Torpedo types include the Type 53-65 passive wake-homing torpedo, and the TEST 71/76 anti-submarine active and passive homing torpedo. It can also launch mines as well as shoulder-launched SAMs.

SPECIFICATIONS

Builder:	Admiralty Shipyard (Sudomekh)
Class:	Sindhugosh (Kilo 877EKM)
Number:	S-62
Mission:	attack submarine
Length:	73m (241ft)
Beam:	9.9m (33ft)
Displacement:	3076 tonnes (3125 tons)
Speed:	17 knots
Operating Depth:	250m (825ft)
Maximum Depth:	330m (1089ft)
Crew:	53
Nuclear Weapons:	none
Conventional Weapons:	533mm (21in) torpedo, SSM
Sonar:	MGK-400 Shark Teeth
Navigation:	MG-519 Snoop Tray
Powerplant:	diesel-electric, 6800 shp
Date Commissioned:	1991

PRIMO LONGOBARDO

The Primo Longobardo class is a fourth-generation batch submarine from the original Sauro class coastal patrol vessel. The class has been modified and adapted over the years, with this class being the most modern of the fleet. Built in Italy in the shipyards of Monfalcone, the Sauro class replaced the submarines of the indigenous Toti class and the American boats of the Romei class. The *Primo Longobardo* diesel-electric attack submarine maintains the same basic design features of the original boats which entered service in 1980, however they have been upgraded technologically. A programme of modernization that started late in 1999 totally reworked the electro-acoustical sensor arrays and the command-and-control suite. The former electro-acoustical system (IPD-70S), the command-and-control system (SACTI MM/BN-716) and the launch and wire-guidance control (FCD Mk 2) system have been removed, and replaced by the ISUS 90-20, an integrated system that can more efficiently perform all the functions formerly managed by the three separate systems. The improvement in performance that the ISUS 90-20 gives also required the sound-dampening technology on the boat to be improved in order to take full advantage of the new suite's capabilities. The ISUS can guide four torpedoes at the same time against four different targets, whilst also managing mines and countermeasures.

SPECIFICATIONS

Builder:	*Italcantieri, Monfalcone*
Class:	*Primo Longobardo*
Number:	*S-524*
Mission:	*coastal patrol submarine*
Length:	*66.3m (219ft)*
Beam:	*6.8m (22ft)*
Displacement:	*1862 tonnes (1891 tons)*
Speed:	*19 knots*
Operating Depth:	*200m (660ft)*
Maximum Depth:	*300m (990ft)*
Crew:	*50*
Nuclear Weapons:	*none*
Conventional Weapons:	*533mm (21in) torpedo, mines*
Sonar:	*ISUS 90-20 sensor suite*
Navigation:	*unknown*
Powerplant:	*diesel-electric, 3650 shp*
Date Commissioned:	*1993*

SALVATORE TODARO

The latest addition to the Italian submarine fleet is the Salvatore Todaro class diesel-electric attack submarine. This class is based on the German designed Type 212A, and the Italian version differs little from the German Navy's. The introduction of the Salvatore Todaro class into the Italian Navy will be a significant step forward for the fleet. The Type 212A is a state-of-the-art diesel submarine, and its capabilities far outreach the Sauro generation of boats. The Salvatore Todaro class will not replace the Sauro generation; indeed, some of the technology from the Type 212A boats will be added to the newest Primo Longobardo class vessels, thus upgrading their capabilities. The Italian-built Type 212A vessels will be constructed by the Fincantieri company at the Monfalcone shipyards. The design is different from the German Type 212A in the life-saving systems on board. The German vessel only has provision for individual escape, whilst the Italian boats have both individual and collective life-saving features. Other than this difference, the two designs are virtually the same and share the same characteristics and capabilities. The areas in which the Salvatore Todaro class will operate are of course different from the German Navy vessels, focusing on the Mediterranean rather than the North Sea and Atlantic, protecting Italy's interests in this theatre.

SPECIFICATIONS

Builder:	Fincantieri/HDW
Class:	Type 212A
Number:	S-526
Mission:	attack submarine
Length:	56m (185ft)
Beam:	7m (23ft)
Displacement:	1830 tonnes (1828ft)
Speed:	20 knots
Operating Depth:	300m (990ft)
Maximum Depth:	400m (1320ft)
Crew:	24
Nuclear Weapons:	none
Conventional Weapons:	533mm (21in) torpedo, Harpoon
Sonar:	Electronik DBQS-40 sonar suite
Navigation:	Kelvin Hughes Type 1007
Powerplant:	diesel-electric AIP, 4243 shp
Date Commissioned:	2005

FUYUSHIO

The Harushio class attack submarine is an indigenously designed and built vessel, and uses a tear-drop type hull, unlike its successor Oyashio class. The design is technically derived from the previous Yushio class and as such there is no major advancement, but instead a few improvements including better silent-running characteristics, a reduction in noise emissions and improvements in underwater manoeuvrability. As is the case with most countries' submarine forces, many exact characteristics of the submarines of the Japanese Maritime Self Defense Force (JMSDF) are not published, with special secrecy concerning maximum depth capabilities. The Harushio class uses the NS110 high-strength steel in portions of the pressure-resistant hull, and the operating depth is presumed to be 300m (990ft) or more, some sources suggesting it to be 500m (1650ft), though this cannot be confirmed. The Harushio class is equipped with the the ZQQ sonar and TASS bow sonar. The torpedo system uses the indigenously designed and built Type 89 torpedoes. The last unit of this class, the *Asashio*, was redesignated as a training submarine (the TSS 3601), and was modified for this role. It was decided in the JMSDF to use a modern vessel as the training platform, so as to model accurately the nature of modern submarine warfare and seamanship.

SPECIFICATIONS

Builder:	*Kawasaki/Mitsubishi*
Class:	*Harushio*
Number:	*SS-588*
Mission:	*attack submarine*
Length:	*77m (254ft)*
Beam:	*10m (33ft)*
Displacement:	*2750 tonnes (2794 tons)*
Speed:	*20 knots*
Operating Depth:	*300m (990ft)*
Maximum Depth:	*400m (1320ft)*
Crew:	*75*
Nuclear Weapons:	*none*
Conventional Weapons:	*533mm (21in) torpedo, Harpoon*
Sonar:	*Hughes/Oki ZQQ-5B sonar suite*
Navigation:	*JRC ZPS 6*
Powerplant:	*diesel-electric, 7200 shp*
Date Commissioned:	*1995*

MAKISHIO

The new Oyashio class attack submarine is an indigenously designed and built vessel that differs from previous submarines of the Japanese Maritime Self Defense Force (JMSDF). Like most submarines, a traditional tear-drop shape hull was the previously preferred design, but the latest and most powerful submarine in the JMSDF inventory has been designed with a "leaf coil" hull form. It incorporates not only a different hull form, but it employs a double-hull system, much like Russian submarines. The design of the Oyashio was built around the arrangement of the sensors first and foremost, after which the entire layout was then built. The traditional method of arrangement placed the most powerful sensors in the bow, but the Oyashio class uses its entire hull as part of the sensor array. In addition, the combat intelligence processing system of the new vessel also improves its attacking capabilities. The position of the torpedo tubes also differs from other similar submarines, with the bow torpedo tubes placement influenced by the arrangement of the sensors. The stealthiness of the hull has been improved by installing anechoic rubber tiles on the hull. High levels of automation throughout the vessel has allowed the number of crew needed to be around 75, thus saving on manpower and the logistics required to support a larger crew.

SPECIFICATIONS

Builder:	Mitsubishi/Kawasaki
Class:	Oyashio
Number:	SS-593
Mission:	attack/patrol submarine
Length:	81.7m (268ft)
Beam:	8.9m (29ft)
Displacement:	3600 tonnes (3657 tons)
Speed:	20 knots
Operating Depth:	300m (990ft)
Maximum Depth:	400m (1320ft)
Crew:	75
Nuclear Weapons:	none
Conventional Weapons:	533mm (21in) torpedo, Harpoon
Sonar:	ZQQ-5B hull/flank arrays
Navigation:	I-band radar system
Powerplant:	diesel-electric, 7700 shp
Date Commissioned:	2001

SACHISHIO

The Yushio class attack submarine represented an enlargement and improvement over the Uzushio class vessels that had preceded it when it was launched in the mid-1970s. A total of 10 were built starting in 1975, and it was the largest class of submarines built for the Japanese Maritime Self Defense Force (JMSDF) at the time. Although it was launched as a second-generation vessel, because the peripheral technology progressed massively over the decade during which they were under construction, the earliest unit and the latter units were almost different types of ships, with the later submarines technologically far superior. Gradual improvements were made over the construction period, and from the fifth boat onward these improvements included the ability to launch the Sub Harpoon missile, and in later units the control navigation system was improved. Type NS80 steel was adopted for the pressure-resistant boat hull, allowing for operations to be carried out safely at depths of approximately 450m (1485ft), though this is unconfirmed officially. Other improvements over its predecessor included the adoption of a seven-bladed propellor, which gave the submarine a reduction in noise emissions. The increase of cruising power, periscope depth range and the large-sized computer conversion of the direction device resulted in a greater war-fighting ability.

SPECIFICATIONS

Builder:	*Kawasaki/Mitsubishi*
Class:	*Yushio*
Number:	*SS-582*
Mission:	*attack submarine*
Length:	*76m (251ft)*
Beam:	*9.9m (33ft)*
Displacement:	*2500 tonnes (2540 tons)*
Speed:	*20 knots*
Operating Depth:	*300m (990ft)*
Maximum Depth:	*400m (1320ft)*
Crew:	*75*
Nuclear Weapons:	*none*
Conventional Weapons:	*533mm (21in) torpedo, Harpoon*
Sonar:	*ZQQ-4 sonar suite*
Navigation:	*ZPS-6 radar*
Powerplant:	*diesel-electric, 7200 shp*
Date Commissioned:	*1989*

HNLMS BRUINVIS

The Walrus 2 class attack submarine is the most modern submarine in the Royal Netherlands Navy (RNLN). The class has been in service since the early 1980s, with the overhauled HNLMS *Bruinvis* representing the last to be launched in 1995. It was brought into service to replace the ageing Zwaardvis class attack vessel. It shares some similarities with its predecessor, having as it does the same general arrangement and hull form as the Zwaardvis 2 class. It also has the same system layout, but differs in having improved diving depth, reduced crew numbers and increased reliability, availability and safety. The operational range of the RNLN submarines lies mainly in the Eastern Atlantic Ocean, the North Sea and the Norwegian Sea, but also in the Mediterranean. Their missions are directed at anti-surface and anti-submarine warfare, carrying out surveillance, special operations and the laying of mines. This modern and sophisticated class contributes an important part to missions nationally and internationally agreed upon, as is the norm for the Dutch armed forces in general. The Dutch Navy takes an active role in participating in NATO naval exercises, and HNLMS *Bruinvis* has taken part in many. She has also recently returned from active duty as part of the US led anti-terrorist operation in Afghanistan, Enduring Freedom.

SPECIFICATIONS

Builder:	Droogdok Maatschappij B.V
Class:	Walrus 2
Number:	S-810
Mission:	attack submarine
Length:	67.7m (223ft)
Beam:	8.4m (28ft)
Displacement:	2800 tonnes (2844 tons)
Speed:	21 knots
Operating Depth:	300m (990ft)
Maximum Depth:	400m (1320ft)
Crew:	49
Nuclear Weapons:	none
Conventional Weapons:	533mm (21in) torpedo, mines
Sonar:	Thomson-Sintra TSM 2272
Navigation:	Signaal/Decca 1229
Powerplant:	diesel-electric, 6200 shp
Date Commissioned:	1994

MORAY

The Moray class submarine is an effort by the Dutch Ministry of Defence to export a number of vessels based on the lessons learnt developing the Walrus and Zwaardvis class submarines. The term Moray stands for Multi Operational Requirement Affected Yield, and the design is essentially a concept framework from which individual buyers can choose the types of systems and configuration of the vessel. The basic hull can be ordered in five different sizes, which although generally retaining the same propulsion and performance, are tailored to varied roles to suit the buyer. The Moray class has six 533mm (21in) torpedo tubes that can launch a variety of weapons including Mk48 torpedoes and the Sub Harpoon surface-to-surface missile, shown above. Despite the potential with the design, however, the Moray has not had many countries interested in the design. The Egyptian Navy was keen on the design and signed a declaration of intent to purchase two boats, but since then progress has stalled. Similarly, Taiwan has expressed an interest in purchasing a number of diesel-electric attack submarines, but due to political difficulties and the Dutch policy of not selling contentious weapons to Taiwan against Chinese wishes this has curbed potential sales. It is a difficult time for submarine manufacturers, and it is uncertain whether the Moray class will ever be bought.

SPECIFICATIONS

Builder:	Droogdok Maatschappij B.V
Class:	Moray 1400 H
Number:	N/A
Mission:	multi-purpose submarine
Length:	64m (211ft)
Beam:	6.4m (21ft)
Displacement:	1800 tonnes (1829 tons)
Speed:	20 knots
Operating Depth:	300m (990ft)
Maximum Depth:	360m (1188ft)
Crew:	32
Nuclear Weapons:	none
Conventional Weapons:	533mm (21in) torpedo, Harpoon
Sonar:	SIASS sonar suite
Navigation:	unknown
Powerplant:	diesel-electric AIP
Date Commissioned:	N/A

ROMEO

The North Korean Navy is the most secretive navy in the world. Determining the state of its fleet is exceptionally difficult and any information is sketchy at best. Even to Western intelligence agencies, names, numbers and bases are not known, and detailed quantities in service are uncertain. This makes determining the Democratic People's Republic of Korea's submarine capabilities extremely difficult. The Romeo class boats operated by the North Korean Navy are indigenously built at either the Nampo or Wonsan shipyards to a 1950s Soviet design. The Romeo class has long been considered obsolete by the Russians, and by modern standards they are archaic in design and capability. Nonetheless, the Romeo class submarines, despite being outdated and slow, are sufficiently capable of blocking sea lanes, but probably only for a limited period. These vessels could also attack South Korea surface vessels, emplace mines anywhere within South Korean maritime territory, or secretly infiltrate commandos into the South. Though North Korea's submarine capability is more readily associated with covert midget submarines, the Romeo class vessels form the backbone of the fleet. There are no plans to replace these aged boats with more modern equivalents, though this is probably down to a lack of funds and the political situation rather than a lack of will.

SPECIFICATIONS

Builder:	Nampo/Wonsan shipyards
Class:	Romeo
Number:	unknown
Mission:	coastal patrol submarine
Length:	76.6m (249ft)
Beam:	6.3m (21ft)
Displacement:	1700 tonnes (1727 tons)
Speed:	13 knots
Operating Depth:	170m (561ft)
Maximum Depth:	unknown
Crew:	50
Nuclear Weapons:	none
Conventional Weapons:	533mm (21in) torpedo, mines
Sonar:	Tamir-5L active
Navigation:	unknown
Powerplant:	diesel-electric, 2700 shp
Date Commissioned:	unknown

SANG-O

The Sang-O class midget submarines of the Democratic People's Republic of Korea Navy are supposedly designed along the lines of the famous Yugoslavian midget submarines. The primary offensive mission of the navy is supporting army actions against South Korea, particularly by inserting small-scale amphibious operations, including special operations forces, along the coast. The Sang-O class boats have also been used in recent years to harass South Korean shipping, though the frequency with which this happens has diminished slightly since the late 1990s. The Sang-O class coastal submarines belong to the Special Naval Infiltration Unit of the Reconnaissance Bureau of the General Staff Department, the Korean People's Army. This Bureau and the Korean Workers' Party's Liaison Office are primarily responsible for intelligence and other covert actions in South Korea. An infiltration team typically numbers three to five men, consisting of two escorts and one to three agents. On insertion missions the escorts are responsible for securing a landing site and then delivering the agents safely ashore. During exfiltration, escorts meet the agents on shore and escort them back to the submarine. How frequently Sang-O boats perform this function is unclear, though a few have been intercepted by Japanese and South Korean forces in recent times.

SPECIFICATIONS

Builder:	Nampo/Wonsan
Class:	Sang-O
Number:	unknown
Mission:	covert infiltration submarine
Length:	35.5m (116ft)
Beam:	3.8m (12ft)
Displacement:	277 tonnes (281 tons)
Speed:	9 knots
Operating Depth:	100m (330ft)
Maximum Depth:	200m (660ft)
Crew:	19 + 6 special operations forces
Nuclear Weapons:	none
Conventional Weapons:	533mm (21in) torpedo, mines
Sonar:	unknown
Navigation:	unknown
Powerplant:	diesel-electric, 800 shp
Date Commissioned:	unknown

YUGO

The Yugo class midget submarine is synonymous with the naval activities of North Korea, yet little is actually known about them. Yugoslavia became synonymous with the design and construction of miniature submarines, and is known to have exported the idea around the world over the decades. In the case of the North Korea Yugo, however, the name Yugo, implying Yugoslav design origin, appears to be a deception, as the vessels appear to bear no resemblance to any of the relatively sophisticated Yugoslav midget submarine designs. Such discoveries have been made in part because of the sporadic capture of these vessels by South Korean warships. North Korea lost another Yugo class saboteur infiltration submarine to operational ineptitude in 1998. According to South Korean sources the craft was found to be of primitive design and without the expected torpedo armament, though it is known that some Yugo submarines are armed with torpedoes. Though the North Korean Navy has a large number of these vessels, some estimates totalling over 50 examples, they are of such a primitive design that in wartime they would stand little chance if discovered by South Korean warships. However, finding such a small craft is difficult even with the most modern sensors, thus one could expect that with a measure of luck, some would get through to deliver their agents.

SPECIFICATIONS

Builder:	unknown
Class:	Yugo
Number:	unknown
Mission:	covert infiltration submarine
Length:	20m (66ft)
Beam:	2m (7ft)
Displacement:	25 tonnes (25.4 tons)
Speed:	4 knots
Operating Depth:	unknown
Maximum Depth:	unknown
Crew:	2 + 7 special operations forces
Nuclear Weapons:	none
Conventional Weapons:	400mm (18in) torpedo
Sonar:	unknown
Navigation:	unknown
Powerplant:	diesel-electric, 160 shp
Date Commissioned:	1960

KNM ULA

The Norwegian Submarine Force consists of six improved Kobben class and six Ula class submarines. Both these classes of vessel are designed for littoral operations and are essentially patrol boats. The Royal Norwegian Navy takes a full and active part in NATO training exercises, and the Ula class recently took part in an extensive exercise in the North Sea called Sorbet Royal 2002. In the wake of the *Kursk* disaster, modern naval operators have begun to explore more rigorously their response doctrines to submarines in distress. During the exercise, the *Utsira*, *Ula*'s sister ship, was deliberately taken to the ocean floor and 18 volunteers of her crew confined to the smallest of the boat's two compartments. Mock rescue operations were then undertaken to rescue these "trapped" crew members. The exercise was a useful experiment in testing NATO's disaster-response doctrine, and the lessons learned will save the lives of any sailors unfortunate enough to be trapped in a sunken submarine. In wartime, the Ula class can gather information on the activities of the enemy, covertly lay mines or can actively destroy the opposition's naval assets. However, in reality the Norwegian Navy will never have to fight without being part of some form of international force, and thus much of its training is geared towards operating effectively with its NATO and UN allies.

SPECIFICATIONS

Builder:	Thyssen Nordseewerke
Class:	Ula
Number:	S-300
Mission:	patrol submarine
Length:	59m (195ft)
Beam:	5.4m (18ft)
Displacement:	1150 tonnes (1168 tons)
Speed:	23 knots
Operating Depth:	unknown
Maximum Depth:	unknown
Crew:	21
Nuclear Weapons:	none
Conventional Weapons:	533mm (21in) torpedo, mines
Sonar:	Atlas Electronik C5U83
Navigation:	Kelvin Hughes Type 1007
Powerplant:	diesel-electric, 1900 shp
Date Commissioned:	1992

PNS HURMAT

The Pakistani Navy acquired two French-built Agosta class attack submarines like the Malaysian Navy one shown above in the late 1970s. They became known as the Hashmat class in Pakistani service. They were originally intended for the South African Navy but were sold to Pakistan before delivery. The procurement of these vessels was a marked leap forward for Pakistan's naval capabilities, since the Agosta submarines were state-of-the-art boats in their day. They have been superceded by the newer Agosta 90Bs, but will remain in Pakistani service for some years to come. Designed and built in the early 1970s, the Agosta class is a versatile and capable diesel-electric submarine. The design was extensively refitted in the late 1980s to fire the Exocet missile. This transformed the Agosta into a ship-killer as well as an anti-submarine vessel, making it sought after by many developing nations. It is a relatively cheap and effective solution, but is now decidedly outdated compared to modern diesel-electric attack submarines. The Pakistani variant of the Agosta is on constant alert, as tensions between Pakistan and its larger neighbour India are almost constantly fraught. Pakistan is continuing in its attempts to procure more modern vessels, obtaining as it has recently the Agosta 90B. However, the Hashmat class is expected to remain in service, but primarily in the patrol role.

SPECIFICATIONS

Builder:	DCN International
Class:	Hashmat (Agosta)
Number:	S-136
Mission:	attack/patrol submarine
Length:	67.6m (223ft)
Beam:	6.8m (22ft)
Displacement:	1725 tonnes (1752 tons)
Speed:	20 knots
Operating Depth:	250m (825ft)
Maximum Depth:	300m (990ft)
Crew:	54
Nuclear Weapons:	none
Conventional Weapons:	533mm (21in) torpedo, Exocet
Sonar:	Thomson DUUA 2 active/passive
Navigation:	Thomson CSF DRUA 33
Powerplant:	diesel-electric, 4600 shp
Date Commissioned:	1980

PNS KHALID

The Agosta 90B class submarine is designed by the French company DCN, and is currently in service with the French, Spanish and Pakistani navies. The Agosta 90B is an improved version of the original Agosta, featuring higher performance and a new combat system. The new submarine features a higher level of automation, which means that the ship's crew has been reduced from 54 to 36 sailors. Other improvements include a new battery for increased range, a deeper diving capability of 350m (1155ft), made possible by the use of HLES 80 steel, and a reduced acoustic signature through the installation of new suspension and isolation systems. Three Agosta 90Bs were ordered by the Pakistani Navy in September 1994. The first, PNS *Khalid*, was built at DCN's Cherbourg yard and was commissioned in 1999. The second, PNS *Saad*, was assembled at Karachi Naval Dockyard and launched in August 2002. The third, PNS *Hamza*, which is being constructed and assembled indigenously at Karachi, is scheduled to be completed by 2005. Work on the vessel was interrupted following a terrorist attack in May 2002, which killed 11 French engineers, but has since restarted. PNS *Hamza* is being fitted with the MESMA Air Independent Propulsion system (AIP). The MESMA AIP system will eventually be retro-fitted to PNS *Khalid* and PNS *Saar*.

SPECIFICATIONS

Builder:	DCN International
Class:	Khalid (Agosta 90B)
Number:	S-137
Mission:	attack submarine
Length:	67.6m (223ft)
Beam:	6.8m (22ft)
Displacement:	1760 tonnes (1788 tons)
Speed:	17 knots
Operating Depth:	300m (990ft)
Maximum Depth:	350m (1155ft)
Crew:	36
Nuclear Weapons:	none
Conventional Weapons:	533mm (21in) torpedo, Exocet
Sonar:	TSM 223 sonar suite
Navigation:	Thales I-band radar
Powerplant:	diesel-electric, 3600 shp
Date Commissioned:	1999

ARKHANGELSK

The Typhoon class boat TK-17 was scheduled to be scrapped, but has recently undergone a year-long refit and is still in active service, expecting to remain so until 2010. The crew petitioned the Navy Headquarters to adopt a new name in July 2002, and it is thus now known as *Arkhangelsk*. This is not an unusual practice in Russian naval circles, as ships can be renamed at any time. This is in stark contrast to most navies around the world. It is a Typhoon class submarine, identical to all the others with the exception that the *Arkhangelsk* is still in operational service. TK-17 was involved in an accident in the Pacific in 1992, where a missile exploded during testing. The *Arkhangelsk* was extensively damaged in the explosion, but has since been repaired. The Typhoon class submarine is of a multi-hulled design. Five inner hulls are situated inside a superstructure of the two parallel main hulls. The superstructure is coated with sound-absorbent tiles. These drastically reduce another submarine's ability to detect the Typhoon. There are 19 compartments, including a strengthened module which houses the main control room and electronic equipment compartment. The design includes features to enable it to both travel under ice sand for ice-breaking. Indeed, a great many of the "cat and mouse" games of the Cold War took place under the polar ice-caps.

SPECIFICATIONS

Builder:	Sevmash
Class:	Typhoon
Number:	TK-17
Mission:	ballistic missile submarine
Length:	172m (564ft)
Beam:	23m (76ft)
Displacement:	2264 tonnes (2300 tons)
Speed:	25 knots
Operating Depth:	350m (1155ft)
Maximum Depth:	500m (1650ft)
Crew:	150
Nuclear Weapons:	20 x SS-N-24 SLBM
Conventional Weapons:	630mm (28in) torpedo, ASROC
Sonar:	Shark Gill sonar suite
Navigation:	unknown
Powerplant:	nuclear reactors, 100,000 shp
Date Commissioned:	1987

AS-19

The Uniform class submarine is a small, deep-diving nuclear submarine. There is not much open source information about this vessel, which suggests that it is used in some form of covert operations, though the manner of which one can only speculate. It is most likely to be employed in "ocean engineering", which is a well-known intelligence euphemism for covert seafloor operations. It is believed to be capable of diving up to depths of well over 910m (3000ft), though obviously precise figures are not available. To achieve this depth it is almost certain that the hull is made of some kind of titanium alloy, perhaps similar to the type used on Sierra class attack submarines. It is also said to be capable of travelling at over 30 knots, which is a remarkable speed for a craft of its size. In addition to its shaft-driven propulsion, the Uniform class is also fitted with side thrusters, which give it high manoeuvrability whilst partaking in its "research", and allows it to hover over one spot. It is unknown whether the Uniform class can disembark any kind of special operations forces, but it would not be too surprising to learn that it did, if that information ever became public. In essence this vessel is probably similar in role to the United States Navy NR-1 deep-diving research vessel, though the AS-19 is much larger, but the reason for its extra size is top secret.

SPECIFICATIONS

Builder:	*United Admiralty Shipyard 196*
Class:	*Uniform*
Number:	*AS-19*
Mission:	*special missions submarine*
Length:	*69m (226ft)*
Beam:	*7m (23ft)*
Displacement:	*1580 tonnes (1605 tons)*
Speed:	*30 knots*
Operating Depth:	*unknown*
Maximum Depth:	*910m (3000ft)*
Crew:	*36*
Nuclear Weapons:	*none*
Conventional Weapons:	*none*
Sonar:	*high-frequency active arrays*
Navigation:	*unknown*
Powerplant:	*nuclear reactor, 6000 shp*
Date Commissioned:	*1995*

AS-35

The Paltus class submarine is the Russian equivalent of the United States Navy NR-1 deep-diving research vessel. It is powered by a small nuclear reactor, but is capable of only six knots. In addition to the main propulsion, it is also fitted with side thrusters to increase its manoeuvrability when on the seafloor. Like the Uniform class deep-diving submarine, the nomenclature of "research vessel" is a little erroneous, because without doubt these vessels are used for covert operations of one form or another. These could include the emplacement of temporary or fixed sensor arrays on the ocean floor and their subsequent maintenance, the investigation of unknown objects, the provision of deep-sea targeting for other vessels or even involvment in rescue operations with stricken submarines. It is also possible that this vessel could deliver special operations forces into highly defended areas. It is believed that the Yankee Stretch conversion of a Yankee class SSBN serves as a mothership for transport and support of these craft, taking them across the vast distances of the oceans before deploying them close to their target areas. This allows the Paltus to be deployed theoretically anywhere in the world at relatively short notice. Numbers of exactly how many Paltus class submarines exist are not readily available; indeed, there may well be only a single craft in service.

SPECIFICATIONS

Builder:	United Admiralty Shipyard 196
Class:	Paltus
Number:	AS-35
Mission:	special missions submarine
Length:	53m (174ft)
Beam:	3.8m (13ft)
Displacement:	730 tonnes (741 tons)
Speed:	6 knots
Operating Depth:	unknown
Maximum Depth:	unknown
Crew:	14
Nuclear Weapons:	none
Conventional Weapons:	none
Sonar:	unknown
Navigation:	1000m (3280ft)
Powerplant:	nuclear reactor, 300 shp
Date Commissioned:	1995

BELGORAD

The Akula II class attack submarine is the latest member of the Akula family to begin entering into service with the Russian Navy. This vessel was the response from the Russian authorities to the realization that US submarines, including the Los Angeles class and the next generation of attack submarines, had the edge over any existing Russian vessel. However, production of the new design has been undertaken at a snail's pace, and there is speculation that the majority of the improved vessels may never see service. The design of the Akula II differs slightly from its predecessors in the fact that it is 4m (13ft) longer. The reason for this is widely believed to be the incorporation of a quieter propulsion system and additional sound-dampening equipment. Furthermore, the Akula II has shifted from being a simple strategic attack submarine to a more general-purpose one. This shift in the doctrine of how the vessel is used means that the breadth of missions that the Akula II can take part in has increased. This is largely driven by the necessity to meet a wide range of potential challenges in an effective yet cost-effective manner. The Akula II lacks none of the required attributes to continue being a formidable submarine, yet the funds needed to alter the operational doctrine and retrain the crews for operations other than anti-submarine actions are decidedly lacking.

SPECIFICATIONS

Builder:	Sevmash
Class:	Akula II
Number:	unknown
Mission:	attack submarine
Length:	112m (369ft)
Beam:	13.5m (45ft)
Displacement:	9500 tonnes (9652 tons)
Speed:	32 knots
Operating Depth:	475m (1570ft)
Maximum Depth:	545m (1800ft)
Crew:	51–62
Nuclear Weapons:	none
Conventional Weapons:	10 x tubes (533mm, 650mm)
Sonar:	MGK Skat, mine detection sonar
Navigation:	Medvyedista-945
Powerplant:	nuclear reactor, 43,000 shp
Date Commissioned:	2001

CHELYABINSK

The Oscar II cruise-missile attack submarine is one of the most advanced of its kind in the world. It is also one of the largest submarines in service, displacing almost 24,000 tonnes (24,384 tons) submerged. During the Cold War, the Soviet Union was deeply afraid of the US aircraft carrier battle groups, and the Oscar class attack submarine was designed to counter this threat. Although the Russian Navy has been forced to scrap large numbers of its submarines, the Oscar II submarines are so important to the Russian Navy that they have received sufficient funds to be maintained in effective operating order. This said, it is believed that three or four vessels are waiting to be scrapped. The Oscar II is more capable than its Oscar I predecessor, and is 10m (33ft) longer, possibly to incorporate a quieter propulsion system. The *Chelyabinsk* is capable of travelling over 30 knots whilst submerged, and carries a compliment of 24 SS-N-19 anti-shipping missiles with a range of 550km (343 miles). The missiles, which are launched while the submarine is submerged in order to achieve surprise and remain undetected, are fired from tubes fixed at an angle of approximately 40 degrees. It can also fire torpedoes and shorter-range anti-shipping missiles from its four 533mm (21in) bow torpedo tubes. The Oscar II class are still awesome submarines.

SPECIFICATIONS

Builder:	*Sevmash*
Class:	*Oscar II*
Number:	*K-442*
Mission:	*cruise-missile submarine*
Length:	*154m (508ft)*
Beam:	*18.2m (60ft)*
Displacement:	*24,000 tonnes (24,384 tons)*
Speed:	*32 knots*
Operating Depth:	*300m (990ft)*
Maximum Depth:	*600m (1980ft)*
Crew:	*94–118*
Nuclear Weapons:	*none*
Conventional Weapons:	*SS-N-19, 533mm (21in) torpedo*
Sonar:	*Shark Gill sonar*
Navigation:	*Snoop Pair radar*
Powerplant:	*nuclear reactor, 90,000 shp*
Date Commissioned:	*1991*

DANIIL MOSKOVSKIY

An improved version of the Victor II, the Victor III was an interim Soviet effort to apply some level of silencing to their submarines. The hull was lengthened by nearly 6m (20ft) to accommodate the rafting and sound insulation for the turbine machinery. The design also features improvements in electronics, navigation systems, and radio and satellite communication systems, accommodated in the additional hull space forward of the sail. All Victor class boats are double-hulled, as is the case in almost all Russian submarines. The outer hull is coated with anti-hydro-acoustic materials to reduce the possibility of detection. The outer hull of the Victor III is made partly from light alloys, and is distinguishable by a high stern fin fitted with a towed array dispenser, the first Soviet submarine to be fitted with a towed array. A total of 26 units were constructed during the Cold War. The Victor class submarines were designed to engage enemy ballistic missile submarines, anti-submarine task forces, and to protect friendly vessels and convoys from enemy attacks. A contemporary of the American Sturgeon class, they were significantly faster but also had much higher noise levels; indeed, the first two designs made no significant effort to reduce noise emissions. Despite its relative age and lack of sophistication, the Victor III is still in service.

SPECIFICATIONS

Builder:	*Admiralty Shipyard*
Class:	*Victor III*
Number:	*K-388*
Mission:	*attack submarine*
Length:	*107m (353ft)*
Beam:	*11m (34ft)*
Displacement:	*7250 tonnes (7366 tons)*
Speed:	*29 knots*
Operating Depth:	*300m (990ft)*
Maximum Depth:	*400m (1320ft)*
Crew:	*85–100*
Nuclear Weapons:	*none*
Conventional Weapons:	*533mm (21in) torpedo, mines*
Sonar:	*Rubikon sonars*
Navigation:	*Medvyedista-671*
Powerplant:	*nuclear reactor, 30,000 shp*
Date Commissioned:	*1984*

DELFIN

The original Kilo Class submarine was designed for anti-submarine and anti-ship warfare in the protection of naval bases, coastal installations and sea lanes, and also for general reconnaissance and patrol missions during the Cold War. Despite its relative age, the Kilo is considered to be one of the quietest diesel submarines in the world. The Project 636 design, which is known in NATO as Improved Kilo, is a generally enhanced development of the original design. The Improved Kilo is actively promoted for the world market by the Rosvoorouzhenie state-owned company, and has been successfully exported to a number of countries including Iran and India. The main differences between the two variations are that the Improved Kilo has better range, firepower, acoustic characteristics and reliability. The hull has also been lengthened by around 1.2m (54in). The Improved Kilo is equipped with six 533mm (21in) forward torpedo tubes situated in the nose of the submarine, and carries 18 torpedoes with 6 in the torpedo tubes and 12 stored on the racks. The submarine can also carry 24 mines with 2 in each of the 6 tubes and 12 on the racks. The Improved Kilo also incorporates a computer-controlled torpedo system with a quick-loading device. It takes only 15 seconds to prepare standby torpedo tubes for firing.

SPECIFICATIONS

Builder:	Admiralty Shipyard
Class:	Improved Kilo
Number:	B-880
Mission:	ASW submarine
Length:	73.8m (242ft)
Beam:	9.9m (32ft)
Displacement:	3126 tonnes (3176 tons)
Speed:	20 knots
Operating Depth:	250m (825ft)
Maximum Depth:	300m (990ft)
Crew:	52
Nuclear Weapons:	none
Conventional Weapons:	533mm (21in) torpedo, mines
Sonar:	Rubikon active/passive sonar
Navigation:	GPS navigation system
Powerplant:	diesel-electric, 5500 shp
Date Commissioned:	1993

KARELIA

The development of the 667BDRM project, more commonly known as the Delta IV class SSBN, ensured that several measures were included to improve its overall capability over its Delta III predecessor. The most significant of these was to reduce its noise level. The gears and equipment were moved and placed on a common base isolated from the pressure hull, and the power compartments were also isolated. The efficiency of the anti-hydro-acoustic coatings of the light outer hull and inner pressure hulls was further improved. A newly designed five-bladed propeller with improved hydro-acoustic characteristics was also introduced. Delta IV submarines are equipped with the TRV-671 RTM missile-torpedo system that has four 533mm (21in) torpedo tubes. Unlike the Delta III, it is capable of using all types of torpedoes, anti-submarine torpedo-missiles and anti-hydro-acoustic devices. The battle-management system, Omnibus-BDRM, controls all combat activities, processes data and commands the torpedo weapons. The Shlyuz navigation system provides for the improved accuracy of the missiles and is capable of stellar navigation at periscope depths. The navigation system also employs two floating antenna buoys to receive radio messages, target destination data and satellite navigation signals at great depth.

SPECIFICATIONS

Builder:	Sevmash
Class:	Delta IV 'Delfin'
Number:	K-18
Mission:	ballistic missile submarine
Length:	167m (551ft)
Beam:	12m (39ft)
Displacement:	18,200 tonnes (18,941 tons)
Speed:	24 knots
Operating Depth:	320m (1056ft)
Maximum Depth:	400m (1320ft)
Crew:	130
Nuclear Weapons:	6 x R-29 RM SLBM
Conventional Weapons:	533mm (21in) torpedo
Sonar:	Skat VDRM
Navigation:	Shlyuz system
Powerplant:	nuclear reactor, 40,000 shp
Date Commissioned:	1991

KASHALOT

The Akula class attack submarine is one of the Russian Navy's most successful and effective weapons systems. Designed and built during the latter years of the Cold War, the Akula was the replacement for the Sierra class submarine. It is made from low-magnetic steel, which was the cheaper and more easily produced alternative to the titanium hull sported by its Sierra class predecessor. This compromised on the diving depth, but was a more practical choice. Like almost all Russian submarines, it is designed with a double hull, in this case with significant distance between the two hulls, giving the inner hull a greater degree of protection in the event of attack. It also has a distinctive aft fin that makes it easily recognizable. Its primary role is to attack surface shipping using either its 533mm (21in) or 650mm (28in) torpedoes, or its SS-N-15 Starfish and SS-N-16 Stallion anti-shipping missiles. It can further attack coastal positions using its Granat cruise missiles which are fired from the 533mm (21in) torpedo tubes. The Akula class can also defend itself from the air with a portable shoulder-launched Strela SA-N-5 surface-to-air missile. This can be fired by a crew member from the deck of the submarine or from the top of the conning tower. The Akula class submarine is a fearsomely armed and powerful vessel, and is still one of the most effective vessels of its kind in the world.

SPECIFICATIONS

Builder:	Sevmash
Class:	Akula
Number:	K-322
Mission:	attack submarine
Length:	108m (356ft)
Beam:	13.5m (45ft)
Displacement:	9100 tonnes (9246 tons)
Speed:	32 knots
Operating Depth:	400m (1320ft)
Maximum Depth:	550m (1800ft)
Crew:	51–62
Nuclear Weapons:	none
Conventional Weapons:	533mm (21in) torpedo, Granat
Sonar:	503-M Skat sonar suite
Navigation:	Medvyedista-945
Powerplant:	nuclear reactor, 43,000 shp
Date Commissioned:	1987

KRAB

The original Sierra I class attack submarine was introduced into Russian service at the height of the Cold War in the mid-1980s, and was seen as a match for the US Los Angeles class submarine. It is generally comparable in performance to early Los Angeles class vessels, though with an arguably superior non-acoustic detection system and integrated acoustic countermeasures system. However, the Improved Los Angeles class boats and subsequent modern designs outstripped the Sierra I's capabilities, and production was switched to the more modern Sierra II class boats. Thus there are only a couple of Sierra Is in service, if indeed they are in operational order. The Sierra design incorporates Cluster Guard anaechoic tiles on the outer hull, which serves to reduce noise levels. Cluster Guard is the official NATO reporting name for sound-absorbing material on newer Soviet submarines. The material is sometimes referred to as tiles because of its block-like configuration, and it is apparently able to reduce the effectiveness of active anti-submarine sonars and active-acoustic torpedo guidance. This technology is featured on almost all newly built submarines, and is seen as an effective countermeasure to the advance of sonar detection systems. The Sierra I was behind the times before it was launched, and is outdated in the twenty-first century.

SPECIFICATIONS

Builder:	Sevmash
Class:	Sierra I
Number:	K-276
Mission:	attack submarine
Length:	107m (353ft)
Beam:	11m (33ft)
Displacement:	10,100 tonnes (10,261 tons)
Speed:	35 knots
Operating Depth:	696m (2300ft)
Maximum Depth:	803m (2650ft)
Crew:	61
Nuclear Weapons:	nuclear depth charges
Conventional Weapons:	533mm (21in) torpedo, mines
Sonar:	Skat sonar suite
Navigation:	Medvyedista-945
Powerplant:	nuclear reactor, 50,000 shp
Date Commissioned:	1987

K-403 YANKEE POD

The K-403 Yankee Pod class submarine is a Yankee class SSBN that has been converted from its ballistic missile role to something more useful for Russia's naval forces. It was subject to the same standard conversion as most of the Yankee class SSBNs, in that it had its missile compartment cut out as part of international arms control agreements. The original Yankee class SSBNs were an integral part of the Soviet Union's nuclear forces, and 34 individual boats served the Russian Navy for over 30 years. They were armed with the R-27 ballistic missile which was able to strike at targets up to 4800km (3000 miles) away. Like the Yankee Stretch, but unlike most Yankee class boats, it was fully converted to another role. This is believed to be as a nuclear-powered trials submarine. It is unclear what experimental weaponry or systems the Yankee Pod has been involved in testing since being commissioned in 1980, which is unsurprising given the nature of the intense secrecy that surrounds submarine operations. However, it is believed that this vessel is currently testing the Irtysh-Amfora sonar suite intended for the new Sevmash class attack submarine. Since a trials submarine is not often subject to the same stresses and strains of fully operational vessels, the Yankee Pod is expected to continue serving as a trials submarine for some time to come.

SPECIFICATIONS

Builder:	Sevmash
Class:	Yankee Pod
Number:	K-403
Mission:	trials submarine
Length:	134m (440ft)
Beam:	12m (39ft)
Displacement:	10,100 tonnes (10,261 tons)
Speed:	27 knots
Operating Depth:	300m (990ft)
Maximum Depth:	400m (1320ft)
Crew:	110
Nuclear Weapons:	none
Conventional Weapons:	none
Sonar:	Irtysh-Amfora sonar suite
Navigation:	Tobol navigation system
Powerplant:	nuclear reactor, 52,000 shp
Date Commissioned:	1980

K-411 YANKEE STRETCH

The K-411 Yankee Stretch submarine is a conversion from a Yankee class SSBN that had been in service with the Russian Navy since 1970. However, as with almost all of the Yankee class boats, K-411 was removed from operational status and her missile compartments cut out to comply with arms control agreement ceilings. Whereas the majority of the Yankee class were decommissioned, a small number were converted. The Yankee Stretch was converted by replacing the missile compartment with an extended hull section. This is widely agreed to be because the K-411 has been extensively modified to serve as the mothership to a very small special operations submarine, the AS-35 Paltus class. The principle is the same as the dry-dock shelter system used by some US submarines, such as the USS *Kamehameha*, in that a larger carrier vessel provides covert support for subaqua special forces operations. This is quite a shift in operational doctrine for the Soviet armed forces, but is a reflection of the efforts being made in the services to meet the new challenges of warfare in the twenty-first century. It is understood that this vessel carries no armament, and is thus reliant on the use of stealth for protection, or it is protected by other armed submarines. It is believed that K-411 is part of the Russian Northern Fleet, and is still operational.

SPECIFICATIONS

Builder:	*Sevmash*
Class:	*Yankee Stretch*
Number:	*K-411*
Mission:	*special missions submarines*
Length:	*160m (525ft)*
Beam:	*12m (39ft)*
Displacement:	*11,600 tonnes (11,785 tons)*
Speed:	*28 knots*
Operating Depth:	*300m (990ft)*
Maximum Depth:	*400m (1320ft)*
Crew:	*110*
Nuclear Weapons:	*none*
Conventional Weapons:	*none*
Sonar:	*unknown*
Navigation:	*Tobol navigation system*
Powerplant:	*nuclear reactors, 52,000 shp*
Date Commissioned:	*1990*

KURSK

The submarine at the heart of one of Russia's most tragic maritime accidents was the Oscar II class cruise missile submarine, K-141 *Kursk*. She sank with all hands after an explosion in her torpedo compartment. Despite early optimism that many of the crew had survived following the explosion, it has since been established that the majority of the crew either died instantly or within hours of the accident. A small number of crewmen did survive the initial explosion but were trapped in the aft of the boat and died shortly from carbondioxide poisoning. Nonetheless, Norwegian and British rescue vessels raced to the scene, but due to inhospitable weather and sea conditions they were unable to achieve any success. On 21 August 2000, Chief of Staff of the Russian Northern Fleet Mikhail Motsak pronounced the *Kursk* flooded and its whole crew dead. As is often the case with such events, claims, counter-claims and conspiracy theories are in abundance. Some Russian sources claim that the *Kursk* was involved in a collision with a US or Royal Navy vessel, or even that the *Kursk* hit a World War II mine, yet an explosion in the torpedo room is now the accepted reason for the *Kursk*'s sinking. The loss of the *Kursk* cast a dark shadow over the entire Russian Navy, and indeed over most of Russian society, and it was seen as the direct result of defence budget cuts.

SPECIFICATIONS

Builder:	*Sevmash*
Class:	*Oscar II*
Number:	*K-141*
Mission:	*cruise-missile submarine*
Length:	*154m (508ft)*
Beam:	*18.2m (60ft)*
Displacement:	*24,000 tonnes (24,384 tons)*
Speed:	*32 knots*
Operating Depth:	*300m (990ft)*
Maximum Depth:	*600m (1980ft)*
Crew:	*94–118*
Nuclear Weapons:	*none*
Conventional Weapons:	*533mm (21in) torpedo, Granat*
Sonar:	*Shark Gill sonar*
Navigation:	*Snoop Pair radar*
Powerplant:	*nuclear reactor, 90,000 shp*
Date Commissioned:	*1994*

NOVOMOSKOVSK

The 667BDRM Delta IV class submarine was constructed parallel to the Typhoon class, and is a follow-on design from its predecessor Delta III class. The Delta IV class is one of Russia's most modern and important submarines. In comparison with the Delta III submarine the diameter of the pressure hull was increased and the bow was lengthened. As a result the displacement of the submarine was increased by 1200 tonnes (1219 tons) and it was lengthened by 12m (39ft). The Delta IV class vessels employ the D-9RM ballistic missile launch system and carry 16 R-29RM liquid-fuelled, submarine-launched ballistic missiles (SLBMs). Each missile carries four multiple independently targetable re-entry vehicles (MIRVs). Each missile is capable of hitting four different targets over 8000km (5000 miles) away, and each of the four MIRV warheads has the explosive power equivalent to over one million tonnes (1.016 million tons) of TNT. There is enough explosive power on a single Delta IV class SSBN to destroy every single state capital in the United States in a matter of minutes. Unlike previous modifications, the Delta IV submarine is able to fire missiles in any direction from a constant course in a circular sector. The underwater firing of the ballistic missiles can be conducted at a depth of 55m (181ft) while cruising at a speed of 6–7 knots.

SPECIFICATIONS

Builder:	Sevmash
Class:	Delta IV
Number:	K-407
Mission:	ballistic missile submarine
Length:	167m (551ft)
Beam:	12m (39ft)
Displacement:	18,200 tonnes (18,941 tons)
Speed:	24 knots
Operating Depth:	320m (1056ft)
Maximum Depth:	400m (1320ft)
Crew:	130
Nuclear Weapons:	16 x R-29 RM SLBM
Conventional Weapons:	533mm (21in) torpedo, mines
Sonar:	Skat VDRM
Navigation:	Shlyuz system
Powerplant:	nuclear reactor, 40,000 shp
Date Commissioned:	1992

PANTERA

The Akula class attack submarine was one of the most feared Russian vessels during the last years of the Cold War. It had been assumed that the Russians could not match the Western powers in terms of technological capability. Whereas this assumption was generally true across most military technical areas, the introduction of the Akula clearly showed that this was not the case for submarines. It came as something of a shock to US intelligence that the Soviet Union had been able to match US technology in its nuclear attack submarines, and the development of the Seawolf class SSN was a direct consequence of the arrival of the Akula class. The Akula is equipped with a sophisticated array of sensors, including the MGK-540 sonar system which provides automatic target detection in broad and narrow band modes by active sonar. It gives the range, relative bearing and range rate. Aside from the less stealthy active sonar, the system can also be used in a passive, listening mode for detection of hostile sonars. The system incorporates a powerful computer that can process and automatically classify targets as well as reject background acoustic noise sources and compensate for the variable acoustic conditions that are prevalent in the sea. The Akula is one of the few classes of boats that have not been left in such disrepair as to render them useless.

SPECIFICATIONS

Builder:	Sevmash
Class:	Akula
Number:	K-317
Mission:	attack submarine
Length:	108m (356ft)
Beam:	13.5m (45ft)
Displacement:	9100 tonnes (9245 tons)
Speed:	32 knots
Operating Depth:	475m (1570ft)
Maximum Depth:	545m (1800ft)
Crew:	51–62
Nuclear Weapons:	none
Conventional Weapons:	533mm (21in) torpedo, Strela
Sonar:	MGK-540 sonar suite
Navigation:	Medvyedista-945
Powerplant:	nuclear reactor, 43,000 shp
Date Commissioned:	1987

PSKOV

The Sierra II class attack submarine was one of Soviet Russia's greatest success stories, and represented the pinnacle of submarine design when it came into service. It was designed as a strategic attack submarine, capable of attacking surface vessels or coastal targets. It was a follow-on from its predecessor, the highly effective Sierra I, and had some major changes made to it in order to improve its capabilities. It differs from the Sierra I in that it has a better sonar system and has a reduced acoustic signature, making it less detectable. It is also around 5m (16.5ft) longer than the Sierra I and also has a larger blunt sail that is 6m (20ft) longer than the Sierra I sail. The increased hull size also provides improved living quarters for the crew and additional sound-dampening measures. It is also equipped with a new American-style spherical bow sonar, a definite break with tradition for the Russian armed forces. The inclusion of this bow sonar meant that there was no room for the torpedo tubes, which were thus moved farther towards the stern and angled out. The torpedo room was also modified to accommodate the Granat strategic cruise missile, giving the Sierra II far greater firepower and capability. As is often the case with specific details about Russian submarines, there is some debate over the number and state of Sierra II vessels still in service.

SPECIFICATIONS

Builder:	*Sevmash*
Class:	*Sierra II*
Number:	*K-534*
Mission:	*attack submarine*
Length:	*113m (372ft)*
Beam:	*12m (40ft)*
Displacement:	*10,400 tonnes (10,566 tons)*
Speed:	*35 knots*
Operating Depth:	*697m (2300ft)*
Maximum Depth:	*803m (2650ft)*
Crew:	*61*
Nuclear Weapons:	*nuclear depth charges*
Conventional Weapons:	*533mm (21in) torpedo, Granat*
Sonar:	*Skat sonar suite*
Navigation:	*Medvyedista-945*
Powerplant:	*nuclear reactor, 50,000 shp*
Date Commissioned:	*1992*

SEVERODVINSK

The Severodvinsk class attack submarine is the latest in the pipeline for the Russian Navy. It is a further derivative of the Akula class attack submarine that has been so successful, and is due to enter service sometime in the next few years. Work on the submarine began in 1992, but there has since then been an ongoing saga over the continued development. Work ceased in 1996 and there is no clear evidence that much has happened since, though estimates state that a budget version of the submarine has been considered as a compromise. US defence analysts have considered that the Severodvinsk class submarine will only be marginally quieter than the existing Akula attack submarine, thus one must question the necessity for another variation given the expense and the state of the Russian Navy. Furthermore, whilst Russian President Vladimir Putin professes a liking for naval matters in public, this is really a public-relations ploy and the fiscal reality is that the navy suffers perhaps more than any other branch of the beleaguered Russian armed forces in terms of underfunding, so there is a chance that the *Severodvinsk* may never be launched. If launched the *Severodvinsk* would be a very capable vessel. In addition to sophisticated sonar, it is designed with eight vertical launch tubes for cruise missiles, as well as four 563mm (25.6in) torpedo tubes.

SPECIFICATIONS

Builder:	Sevmash
Class:	Severodvinsk
Number:	none currently assigned
Mission:	attack submarine
Length:	111m (333ft)
Beam:	12m (40ft)
Displacement:	13,000 tonnes (13,208 tons)
Speed:	30 knots
Operating Depth:	455m (1500ft)
Maximum Depth:	606m (2000ft)
Crew:	50
Nuclear Weapons:	none
Conventional Weapons:	563mm (25.6in) torpedo, Granat
Sonar:	Irtysh-Amfora sonar suite
Navigation:	Myedvyeditsa-971
Powerplant:	nuclear reactor, 43,000 shp
Date Commissioned:	unknown

SEVERSTAL

The Typhoon ballistic missile nuclear-powered submarines are the largest submarines ever to be built, and were a defining feature of the Cold War. They were constructed at the Sevmash shipyard, on the White Sea near Archangel. The Typhoon class submarine is of multi-hulled design with five inner hulls situated inside a superstructure of the two parallel main hulls. The super-structure is coated with sound-absorbent tiles. There are 19 compartments, including a strengthened module which houses the main control room and electronic equipment compartment, which is above the main hulls behind the missile launch tubes. Maximum diving depth is officially 500m (1650ft), though it could be significantly more. The Typhoon class carries 20 of the RSM-52 intercontinental ballistic missiles designed by the Makayev Design Bureau. The NATO designation for the weapon is the SS-N-20 Sturgeon. Each missile consists of 10 independently targetable multiple re-entry vehicles (MIRVs), each with a 100 kiloton nuclear warhead. The missile has a range of 8300km (5100 miles) and is able to hit its target within 500m (1650ft). The Typhoon class has four 630mm (28in) torpedo tubes and two 533mm (21in) torpedo tubes, with a total of 22 anti-ship missiles and torpedoes of varying types. Though slated to be scrapped, the *Severstal* is still in service.

SPECIFICATIONS

Builder:	*Sevmash*
Class:	*Typhoon*
Number:	*TK-20*
Mission:	*ballistic missile submarine*
Length:	*172m (564ft)*
Beam:	*23m (76ft)*
Displacement:	*33,800 tonnes (34,340 tons)*
Speed:	*25 knots*
Operating Depth:	*350m (1155ft)*
Maximum Depth:	*500m (1650ft)*
Crew:	*150*
Nuclear Weapons:	*20 x SS-N-24 SLBM*
Conventional Weapons:	*630mm (28in) torpedo, ASROC*
Sonar:	*Shark Gill sonar suite*
Navigation:	*unknown*
Powerplant:	*nuclear reactor, 100,000 shp*
Date Commissioned:	*1989*

SYVATOY GIORGIY

The development of the 667BDR Delta III ballistic missile submarine began in 1972 at the Rubin Central Design Bureau for Marine Engineering. This strategic submarine is equipped with the D-9R launch system and 16 SS-N-18 missiles, and was the first submarine to be able to fire any number of missiles in a single salvo. The SS-N-18 missile was the first sea-based Soviet ballistic missile, each carrying 3–7 multiple independently targetable re-entry vehicles (MIRVs), with a range of up to 8000km (5000 miles) depending on the number of MIRVs deployed. The Delta III is equipped with the Almaz-BDR battle-management system and the Tobol-M2 inertial navigation system. The Delta III is also equipped with the Rubikon hydro-acoustic system. The Delta III SSBNs entered service in 1976, and by 1982 a total of 14 submarines were commissioned, all built at Sevmash shipyards. The operational lifetime of these submarines is estimated to be 20–25 years, so they are getting a little long in the tooth. In terms of capability the Delta III is behind its more modern counterparts, though the Russian Navy still retains a small number of these vessels, most of which are in reserve. There are no precise figures available in open-source intelligence as to how many Delta IIIs are still in operational order, though estimates put the number as low as four.

SPECIFICATIONS

Builder:	Sevmash
Class:	Delta III
Number:	K-433
Mission:	ballistic missile submarine
Length:	155m (511ft)
Beam:	11.7m (38ft)
Displacement:	10,600 tonnes (10,796 tons)
Speed:	24 knots
Operating Depth:	320m (1056ft)
Maximum Depth:	400m (1320ft)
Crew:	130
Nuclear Weapons:	16 x SS-N-18 SLBM
Conventional Weapons:	533mm (21in) torpedo, Vodopod
Sonar:	Rubikon sonar suite
Navigation:	Tobol M-2
Powerplant:	nuclear reactor, 60,000 shp
Date Commissioned:	1981

TIGR

The Akula class attack submarine has undergone a series of improvement refits and upgrades since its introduction. The first of these takes the Akula up to the Improved Akula I class. This vessel does not differ extensively from the Akula, but it does have a number of improvements. Along with the pre-existing six 630mm (28in) torpedo tubes, the upgrade includes the addition of two extra 533mm (21in) torpedo tubes to the existing compliment of four tubes, taking the number of available tubes to 10. This gives the Improved Akula I an awesome amount of firepower. There are only a handful of Improved Akula Is in the Russian Navy, with some estimates reckoning on only five or six boats split between the Northern and Pacific fleets. There are also rumoured to be improvements in the sound-dampening equipment in the Improved Akula, making it marginally quieter than the original. The vessel is at its quietest at a speed of 6–9 knots, but it is still not as quiet as the US Los Angeles class attack submarine at higher speeds. There is some debate amongst those who keep a close eye on Russian submarine developments about what the difference is between an Improved Akula and the Akula II. Ultimately it is difficult to tell since the majority of alterations on each version are in the heart of the vessel, obscured from view.

SPECIFICATIONS

Builder:	Sevmash
Class:	Improved Akula
Number:	K-157
Mission:	attack submarine
Length:	108m (356ft)
Beam:	13.5m (45ft)
Displacement:	9100 tonnes (9245 tons)
Speed:	32 knots
Operating Depth:	475m (1570ft)
Maximum Depth:	545m (1800ft)
Crew:	51–62
Nuclear Weapons:	none
Conventional Weapons:	630mm (28in) torpedo
Sonar:	Skat, MG-70 mine detection
Navigation:	Medvyedista-945
Powerplant:	nuclear reactor, 43,000 shp
Date Commissioned:	1994

VLADIKAVKAZ

The Kilo class submarine is a standard Soviet diesel-electric submarine design, which has also been produced extensively for export. It was designed with general coastal/littoral operations in mind, as opposed to deep-water operations. Despite the age of the design, and the improvements made to its Improved Kilo successor, the Kilo is still considered to be a very quiet vessel. The Russian Navy still has a number of Kilo class submarines in service, with estimates ranging around 14 on operational duty, and a further 7 in reserve, though the mix of standard and Improved Kilos is not known. The Russian fleet operates three variants of the Kilo, known as project 877: the basic 877, the 877K that has an improved fire-control system, and the 877M that can fire wire-guided torpedoes from two tubes. Though the Kilo class is no longer in production for the Russian Navy, it continues to be popular with other nations. The Kilo class has been a very successful export for the Russian Navy, and continues to generate a decent amount of much-needed income for the failing Russian economy. Since each unit costs around $90 million US and at least 21 vessels have been sold to foreign governments, including 10 units to India, 4 to China, 3 to Iran and 2 to Algeria, it suggests that almost $2 billion US has been raised through foreign export sales.

SPECIFICATIONS

Builder:	Sevmash
Class:	Kilo
Number:	B-459
Mission:	ASW submarine
Length:	72.6m (238ft)
Beam:	9.9m (32ft)
Displacement:	2450 tonnes (2489 tons)
Speed:	17 knots
Operating Depth:	240m (792ft)
Maximum Depth:	300m (990ft)
Crew:	53
Nuclear Weapons:	none
Conventional Weapons:	533mm (21in) torpedo
Sonar:	Rubikon sonar suite
Navigation:	GPS-based navigation system
Powerplant:	diesel-electric, 5900 shp
Date Commissioned:	unknown

YURIY DOLGORUKIY

The *Yuri Dolgorukiy* is a Borei class fourth-generation SSBN and was laid down at the Sevmash State Nuclear Shipbuilding Centre (shown above) at Sevmash in November 1996. The city of Moscow is sponsoring the project, as the lead vessel is named after Prince Dolgorukiy, the traditional founder of the city. So-called "presentation weapons" were commonplace in the Red Army during the Great Patriotic War. Presentation weapons were almost always the result of monetary collections taken up locally and voluntarily, and offered towards the cost of various vehicles or other items in the name of some personality or entity. Thus, the workers of a factory, town, or even just local citizens could take up a collection and buy a tank or aircraft in the name of their factory, group or a local figure. The Borei class will carry 20 SLBMs of a new type, yet the new SLBM has not yet been designed, which is a major reason for the delay in the completion of the first vessel. The intended missile, SS-N-28, failed its testing phase and was abandoned, and no replacement has been found. The lead unit of Russia's fourth-generation ballistic missile submarine would have reached initial operational capability by 2004, if the current plan of launching it by 2002 had remained on track. Suffice to say this has not happened, and the future of the project is unclear.

SPECIFICATIONS

Builder:	Sevmash
Class:	Borei
Number:	955
Mission:	ballistic missile submarine
Length:	170m (561ft)
Beam:	13.5m (45ft)
Displacement:	19,000 tonnes (19,400 tons)
Speed:	29 knots
Operating Depth:	unknown
Maximum Depth:	unknown
Crew:	110
Nuclear Weapons:	New SLBM
Conventional Weapons:	533mm (21in) torpedo
Sonar:	MGK-540 Skat-3M sonar suite
Navigation:	unknown
Powerplant:	nuclear reactors, 98,000 shp
Date Commissioned:	2005

ROKS LEE JONG MOO

The addition of the popular Type 209 German-designed attack submarine to the Republic of Korea Navy is part of an extensive expansion and modernization of its armed forces. The Changbogo class submarines, as the Type 209/1200 has been christened, are diesel-electric propulsion submarines, built under license in South Korea by the Daewoo company. ROKS *Changbogo*, the first ship of this class, was launched in June 1992 by HDW at their Kiel shipyards and commissioned in 1993. The second and subsequent boats were built by Daewoo Heavy Industries at Koje island, South Korea. The Changbogo class boats are far more sophisticated than any vessel in the North Korean fleet, and though North Korea has an advantage in terms of sheer numbers, they are old and often in poor condition. The covert incursion of North Korean submarines into South Korean territory on a frequent basis certainly keep the submariners of the ROK Navy busy and well-trained. According to the ROK naval doctrine, "The mission of the navy during peacetime is not only to deter war, but also to protect national and maritime sovereignty. Its mission during war is to guarantee the safety of our activities at sea by protecting the sea lines of communications, the life line of the country." The addition of the modern Changbogo class vessels goes a long way to fulfiling this strategic doctrine.

SPECIFICATIONS

Builder:	*Daewoo Heavy Industries*
Class:	*Changbogo (Type 209/1200)*
Number:	*SS-066*
Mission:	*attack submarine*
Length:	*56m (187ft)*
Beam:	*6.2m (20ft)*
Displacement:	*1264 tonnes (1285 tons)*
Speed:	*22 knots*
Operating Depth:	*250m (825ft)*
Maximum Depth:	*300m (990ft)*
Crew:	*30*
Nuclear Weapons:	*none*
Conventional Weapons:	*533mm (21in) torpedo, mines*
Sonar:	*CSU 83 sonar suite*
Navigation:	*Raytheon SPS-10C radar*
Powerplant:	*diesel-electric, 5900 shp*
Date Commissioned:	*1998*

NARVAL

The Delfin class patrol boat used by the Spanish Navy is a French-designed Daphne class vessel, but built under license in Spain with some modifications to the original design. This class of boat has been in operational service with the Spanish Navy for over 30 years, and is thus coming to the end of its operational life. Indeed, by some standards 30 years is an exceptionally long period of time for an attack submarine to remain in service given the advances in technology and computerization. In Spanish service, the Delfin class is scheduled to be replaced by the new Scorpène class very shortly, though as with many submarine-building projects around the world, the Scorpène class is behind schedule. Built in the 1950s through to the 1970s, the Daphne is a common attack submarine throughout the world. Of a simple conventional layout, the Daphne is a standard submarine, save the four aft torpedo tubes, which means that is has some measure of protection whilst retreating, or if it is caught unawares. However, this type of design shows the age of the boat and the era from which it came, since modern submarines do not generally incorporate a dedicated set of aft-facing torpedo tubes because they are considered redundant. The *Narval* represents the last of the original batch of Delfin submarines, and is being withdrawn from service in 2005.

SPECIFICATIONS

Builder:	ENB Cartagena Shipbuilding
Class:	Delfin (Daphne)
Number:	S-64
Mission:	attack/patrol submarine
Length:	57.6m (190ft)
Beam:	6.7m (22ft)
Displacement:	1043 tonnes (1060 tons)
Speed:	15 knots
Operating Depth:	200m (660ft)
Maximum Depth:	300m (990ft)
Crew:	56
Nuclear Weapons:	none
Conventional Weapons:	533mm (21in) torpedo, mines
Sonar:	Thomson Sintra DSUV 22A
Navigation:	unknown
Powerplant:	diesel-electric, 2000 shp
Date Commissioned:	1975

SCORPÈNE

The Spanish Navy has agreed to procure a number of Scorpène class attack submarines to replace its ageing Dolfin class boats. The class is derived from a family of advanced submarines designed by the French company DCN for export purposes, utilizing the technologies used in the French Navy's latest SSNs and SSBNs. There are three different types of Scorpène design, with the Spanish choice being the largest of the three which incorporates an Air Independent Propulsion (AIP) system. The Scorpène class is equipped with six bow-located 533mm (21in) torpedo tubes able to launch a variety of torpedoes, as well as surface-to-surface missiles. Up to 18 torpedoes and missiles can be carried, or 30 mines. The loading of weapons is automated, thus reducing the number of crew needed. The sonar suite includes a long-range passive cylindrical array, an intercept sonar, active sonar, distributed array, flank array, and a high-resolution sonar for mine and obstacle avoidance. The key planning concepts for the Scorpène class were to design an extremely quiet vessel with great detection capabilities and offensive power for missions ranging from anti-submarine and anti-surface warfare to special operations and intelligence gathering. Thus the Spanish Navy has invested in a submarine capable of providing it with excellent capabilities well into the twenty-first century.

SPECIFICATIONS

Builder:	Izar Cartagena Shipbuilding
Class:	S-80 Scorpène
Number:	S-80
Mission:	patrol/attack submarine
Length:	66.4m (219ft)
Beam:	6.2m (21ft)
Displacement:	1565 tonnes (1590 tons)
Speed:	20 knots
Operating Depth:	270m (891ft)
Maximum Depth:	350m (1155ft)
Crew:	33
Nuclear Weapons:	none
Conventional Weapons:	533mm (21in) torpedo, SSM
Sonar:	SUBTICS combat system
Navigation:	Kelvin-Hughes Type 1007
Powerplant:	diesel-electric AIP, 3800 shp
Date Commissioned:	2005

SIROCO

The Galerna coastal patrol submarine is a derivative of the French-designed and built Agosta class boat. As with all of the Spanish Navy's submarines, with the exception of the Scorpène class, the Galerna is a French submarine but built indigenously by the ENB Cartagena Shipbuilding Company, with improved electronic equipment. The original Agosta class was introduced into service in the 1970s, with an extensive refit taking place in the early 1990s to prolong the service life of the class, and make it more capable. This refit tailored the boats to fire the Exocet anti-shipping missile in addition to torpedoes. The Galerna class is used by the Spanish Navy primarily as a coastal patrol submarine, and thus it is not outfitted to be especially effective in deep-water environments. However, despite its limitations it is an effective weapons platform in littoral operations, and carries a formidable array of weapons for a vessel of its size. The Agosta class is currently in service with the French, Spanish and Pakistan navies. Four Galerna submarines were entered into service with the Spanish Navy during the mid-1980s, and all four remain on active duty. Their responsibilities include patrolling Spain's coastal areas, as well as its fishing territories. They can monitor the shipping coming in and out of Spanish waters, and challenge any vessels attempting to fish illegally or smuggle goods.

SPECIFICATIONS

Builder:	ENB Cartagena Shipbuilding
Class:	Galerna
Number:	S-72
Mission:	coastal patrol submarine
Length:	67.6m (223ft)
Beam:	6.8m (22ft)
Displacement:	1767 tonnes (1795 tons)
Speed:	20 knots
Operating Depth:	250m (825ft)
Maximum Depth:	300m (990ft)
Crew:	50
Nuclear Weapons:	none
Conventional Weapons:	533m (21in) torpedo, Exocet
Sonar:	DUUX-5
Navigation:	Thomson-CSF DRUA 33
Powerplant:	diesel-electric, 4600 shp
Date Commissioned:	1984

HMS NEPTUN

The Nacken class submarine is a fairly common diesel-electric boat, and is small and quiet, allowing for littoral warfare. As with the other diesel boats, the Nacken class is not an especially capable ocean-going vessel, but is instead designed for littoral operations. All the vessels of this class, a total of only two boats, have had their electronics and combat systems upgraded to the same standard as the Vastergotland class. The class is armed with eight torpedo tubes consisting of six 533mm (21in) tubes and two 400mm (15.7in) tubes. They can carry a total of 12 torpedoes, with 8 held in the tubes and the other 4 on the racks. The first-of-class vessel from which the class derives its name, HMS *Nacken,* is no longer in Swedish service. It was outfitted with the new Stirling Air Independent Propulsion (AIP) system and used as the test-bed for the next-generation Gotland class attack submarine. It was very successful in this role, and on the strength of its performance attracted admirers from other Scandinavian naval forces. After it was agreed that HMS *Nacken* could be sold with the AIP system, Denmark put in an offer for the boat. It was then subsequently sold to the Danish Navy with the AIP system intact, and was renamed *Kronborg.* The two remaining boats are still in Swedish service, but will be mothballed once the Gotland procurement is complete.

SPECIFICATIONS

Builder:	Kockums
Class:	Nacken
Number:	A-16
Mission:	patrol/attack submarine
Length:	49.5m (162ft)
Beam:	5.7m (19ft)
Displacement:	1145 tonnes (1163 tons)
Speed:	20 knots
Operating Depth:	250m (825ft)
Maximum Depth:	300m (990ft)
Crew:	19
Nuclear Weapons:	none
Conventional Weapons:	533mm (21in) torpedo, mines
Sonar:	Atlas CSU-83 sonar suite
Navigation:	Terma radar
Powerplant:	diesel-electric, 1500 shp
Date Commissioned:	1981

HMS OSTERGOTLAND

The Sodermanland class attack submarine is an improved version of the original Vastergotland class submarine that has been the Swedish Navy's premier attack vessel since the late 1980s. Despite its relatively small size it is a capable weapons platform. In terms of technology the Sodermanland is easily outclassed by the new Gotland boats, but it will remain in service. This is due to the fact that the final two boats of the Vastergotland class will be fitted with the Stirling Air Independent Propulsion(AIP) system that is fitted to the Gotland class, and renamed the Sodermanland class. The conversion is an extensive operation. The submarines will be cut in two immediately aft of the tower and lengthened by the insertion of the Stirling AIP section. This section, fully fitted and equipped before installation, contains two Stirling units, liquid oxygen (LOX) tanks and electrical equipment. The inclusion of this section increases the length by almost 12m (40ft). The first boat to be converted is the *Sodermanland*, which will be relaunched in 2003, and the *Ostermanland* will be relaunched in 2004. Another aspect of the class conversion is that the submarines will be equipped to undertake international peacekeeping missions in warmer and more saline waters. This conversion includes the addition of different filtration systems and heating/cooling apparatus.

SPECIFICATIONS

Builder:	*Kockums*
Class:	*Sodermanland*
Number:	*unknown*
Mission:	*patrol/attack submarine*
Length:	*60.5m (200ft)*
Beam:	*6.1m (20ft)*
Displacement:	*1500 tonnes (1524 tons)*
Speed:	*20 knots*
Operating Depth:	*300m (990ft)*
Maximum Depth:	*400m (1320ft)*
Crew:	*30*
Nuclear Weapons:	*none*
Conventional Weapons:	*533mm (21in) torpedo, SSM*
Sonar:	*Atlas Electronik CSU83 sonar suite*
Navigation:	*Terma radar*
Powerplant:	*diesel-electric, 1800 shp*
Date Commissioned:	*1990 (relaunched 2004)*

HMS UPPLAND

The Gotland class attack submarine is the latest addition to the Royal Swedish Navy's submarine fleet, having been in service since 1997. This class is essentially an improved version of its predecessor, the Vastergotland class, and is one of the world's most modern conventionally powered submarines, and one of the finest. It is capable of achieving a variety of missions, such as anti-shipping operations, anti-submarine missions, forward surveillance, special operations and minelaying. During wartime, the Gotland class would be employed to gather intelligence on the enemy, lay mines close to the coast to deter invasion, and harass enemy vessels. To achieve this, these submarines can carry a powerful array of wire-guided and homing torpedoes, missiles and mines. Saab Bofors Underwater Systems has developed a new heavyweight torpedo for the Swedish Navy, the Torpedo 2000, built with the Gotland submarines in mind. It is a high-speed anti-submarine/anti-surface torpedo with a range of more than 40km (25 miles) and a speed of over 40 knots. The Gotland class was also the world's first conventional submarine originally designed with an Air Independent Propulsion (AIP) system. Other conventional submarines have begun to incorporate this cutting-edge technology, but the Gotland was the first to enter active service.

SPECIFICATIONS

Builder:	Kockums HDW
Class:	Gotland
Number:	A-20
Mission:	attack submarine
Length:	60m (199ft)
Beam:	6.2m (20ft)
Displacement:	1500 tonnes (1524 tons)
Speed:	20 knots
Operating Depth:	300m (990ft)
Maximum Depth:	450m (1485ft)
Crew:	25
Nuclear Weapons:	none
Conventional Weapons:	533mm (21in) torpedo, Harpoon
Sonar:	Atlas Electronik CSU 90-2 sonar
Navigation:	Terma Scanter navigation radar
Powerplant:	diesel-electric AIP
Date Commissioned:	1997

HMS VASTERGOTLAND

The Vastergotland class attack submarine has been the Swedish Navy's primary "hunter-killer" submarine since the late 1980s. Despite having been left behind technologically by the new Gotland class and improved Sodermanland class boats, it is still a capable weapons platform. The class is fitted with nine torpedo tubes; six bow mounted 533mm (21in) tubes, and three aft mounted 400mm (15.7in) tubes. They can launch two different calibres of torpedo, the type 613 heavyweight torpedo, and the type 431/451 lightweight torpedo. It can also place mines in lieu of carrying torpedoes. The Vastergotland class operates almost exclusively in the cold waters of the North Sea and northern Atlantic, as well as in the Baltic Sea. Though they are not especially old vessels, they will be placed in reserve once all the Gotland and Sodermanland class boats have entered service. The advanced capabilities of these two classes means that the original Vastergotland class is unable to match them operationally, and thus the cost of maintaining them is not warranted. If a state of war was to break out, however, the two mothballed vessels would be able to be brought back into service within a very short space of time. Whether there would be the manpower and expertise needed to operate them effectively is debatable. In reality, though, there is little chance they will be needed.

SPECIFICATIONS

Builder:	*Kockums*
Class:	*Vastergotland*
Number:	*A-17*
Mission:	*patrol/attack submarine*
Length:	*48.5m (160ft)*
Beam:	*6.1m (20ft)*
Displacement:	*1143 tonnes (1161 tons)*
Speed:	*20 knots*
Operating Depth:	*300m (990ft)*
Maximum Depth:	*400m (1320ft)*
Crew:	*30*
Nuclear Weapons:	*none*
Conventional Weapons:	*533mm (21in) torpedo, Harpoon*
Sonar:	*Atlas Electronik CSU-83 sonar*
Navigation:	*Terma radar*
Powerplant:	*diesel-electric, 1800 shp*
Date Commissioned:	*1988*

HAI HU

The story of Taiwanese attempts to procure or produce good-quality conventionally powered submarines is one of the ongoing sagas of the international arms trade. Taiwan has long been in the market for additional diesel submarines to counter China's growing naval might. Under its proposed submarine programme, Taiwan's navy plans to increase its submarine fleet to 12 vessels. But Taiwan's desires to add new submarines to the navy have tended to move no further than paper agreements. The main submarine exporters, such as Germany and the United States, have not endorsed Taiwan's proposals because of fears it could upset the balance between the Chinese mainland and Taiwan, and provoke an international crisis. This fear is not without grounds, since China downgraded its diplomatic relations with the Netherlands following the sale of the two Zwaardvis boats to Taiwan in the late 1980s. Thus Taiwan's navy currently has only four submarines, two of which are too old for operations and are used only as training vessels. The remaining two are the Dutch vessels. During hostilities, these two Hai Lung class submarines could be used to protect Taiwan's shipping lanes and ports, preventing them from being mined, or could even take on offensive operations and attack enemy shipping and mine the enemy's ports with a compliment of torpedoes, mines and missiles.

SPECIFICATIONS

Builder:	Wilton Fijenoord
Class:	Hai Lung (Zwaardvis)
Number:	794
Mission:	attack/patrol submarine
Length:	66.9m (219ft)
Beam:	8.4m (27ft)
Displacement:	2660 tonnes (2702 tons)
Speed:	20 knots
Operating Depth:	240m (792ft)
Maximum Depth:	300m (990ft)
Crew:	67
Nuclear Weapons:	none
Conventional Weapons:	533mm (21in) torpedo, SSM
Sonar:	Signaal SIASS-Z sonar suite
Navigation:	Signaal ZW-07
Powerplant:	diesel-electric, 5100 shp
Date Commissioned:	1988

TCG ANAFARTALAR

The Preveze class attack submarine is the Turkish Navy's version of the German-designed Type 209 submarine from the well-known ship designers HDW. It is also the latest addition to their submarine fleet. The Anafartalar is the enlarged Type 209/1400 version, which displaces slightly more than its Atilay class predecessor. The Turkish Navy has ordered an additional number of these boats to supplement an already impressive submarine force. Though the Turkish Navy still operates some ancient World War II Guppy class submarines, the new Type 209 Preveze class will make its fleet more modern and enhance its military capabilities many times. This class of boat is designed for coastal patrol and attack missions in littoral environments, rather than blue-water operations. The chief theatre of operations for the Turkish Navy is in and around the Mediterranean, with occasional expeditions into the Atlantic and elsewhere. A prime task of the submarine force is to secure Turkey's vital shipping lanes, since the country depends heavily on its freedom to import and export goods via giant cargo ships without fear of sabotage. Furthermore, Turkish submarines take part in the constant ritual of spying on its traditional enemy, Greece. Aside from monitoring Greek naval manoeuvres, the Type 209 vessels continue the vigil on the divided island of Cyprus.

SPECIFICATIONS

Builder:	Gölcük Naval Yard
Class:	Preveze (Type 209/1400)
Number:	S-365
Mission:	attack submarine
Length:	62m (204ft)
Beam:	6.2m (20ft)
Displacement:	1586 tonnes (1611 tons)
Speed:	21 knots
Operating Depth:	300m (990ft)
Maximum Depth:	350m (1155ft)
Crew:	30
Nuclear Weapons:	none
Conventional Weapons:	533mm (21in) torpedo, Harpoon
Sonar:	CSU-81/1 sonar suite
Navigation:	unknown
Powerplant:	diesel-electric, 5000 shp
Date Commissioned:	1999

TCG DOLUNAY

The Turkish Navy's Atilay class attack submarine is a close relation to its Preveze class cousin. The class, of which TCG *Dolunay* is one, is an older Type 209/1200 submarine from the same German designers that delivered the Preveze class, Howaldswerke-Deutsche Werft (HDW). The introduction of the original Type 209s in the mid-1970s signalled a new era for the Turkish submarine fleet. The contract between the German shipbuilders and the Turkish Navy agreed that the first batch of three submarines would be built at Kiel by HDW, whilst the remaining boats would be built with German assistance at the Gölcük shipyards in Turkey. The type proved so successful that the Preveze class was ordered on the strength of the Atilay's performance, and the relationship between the Turkish Navy and HDW has seen a second batch of Type 209/1400 Preveze class ordered. The generic Type 209/1200 is designed as a coastal submarine with anti-submarine and anti-surface ship warfare in mind, along with the protection of naval bases, coastal installations and sea lanes, and also for general reconnaissance and patrol missions. The vessel is armed with eight 533mm (21in) torpedo tubes, and is able to fire the AEG SST-4 torpedo, of which it carries 14, as well as other types of mines and countermeasures. It cannot fire surface-to-surface missiles however.

SPECIFICATIONS

Builder:	Gölcük Naval Yard
Class:	Atilay (Type 209/1200)
Number:	S-352
Mission:	attack submarine
Length:	55.9m (183ft)
Beam:	6.3m (21ft)
Displacement:	1285 tonnes (1306 tons)
Speed:	22 knots
Operating Depth:	250m (825ft)
Maximum Depth:	350m (1155ft)
Crew:	33
Nuclear Weapons:	none
Conventional Weapons:	533mm (21in) torpedo, mines
Sonar:	CSU-3 sonar suite
Navigation:	unknown
Powerplant:	diesel-electric, 5000 shp
Date Commissioned:	1990

ASTUTE

The new Astute class submarine is the United Kingdom's latest nuclear powered hunter-killer attack submarine, designed to replace the ageing Swiftsure class. Though based on the Trafalgar class, indeed they were originally known as Batch 2 Trafalgar, they are a major upgrade with an extensively modified front hull. When the Astute class comes into operation in 2006, it will be one of the most capable submarines anywhere in the world. As with all first-rate military powers, the United Kingdom has had to adapt its military doctrine to embrace the new concepts of warfare. Thus the Astute class has been designed with flexibility in mind, able to operate in many different environments at short notice, and use its full compliment of sophisticated weaponry and systems to aid any particular task force. There exists an order for the first batch of three Astute class submarines to be delivered in the first decade of the twenty-first century, and BAE Systems Marine, the prime contractor, expects another order of three to be placed. The Astute is equipped with the Tomahawk Block III cruise missile (TLAM) from US company Raytheon and the Sub Harpoon anti-shipping missile produced by Boeing. Both are fired from 533mm (21in) torpedo tubes. Also carried is the Spearfish torpedo, which has a range is 65km (40 miles).

SPECIFICATIONS

Builder:	*BAE Systems Marine*
Class:	*Astute*
Number:	*unknown*
Mission:	*attack submarine*
Length:	*91.7m (303ft)*
Beam:	*10.4m (34ft)*
Displacement:	*7200 tonnes (7315 tons)*
Speed:	*29 knots*
Operating Depth:	*300m (990ft)*
Maximum Depth:	*400m (1320ft)*
Crew:	*110*
Nuclear Weapons:	*none*
Conventional Weapons:	*533mm (21in) torpedo, TLAM*
Sonar:	*Thales 2076 sonar suite*
Navigation:	*I-band radar suite*
Powerplant:	*nuclear reactor, 15,000 shp*
Date Commissioned:	*2006*

HMS SOVEREIGN

The ageing Swiftsure class attack submarine was built and added to the Royal Navy's submarine fleet to supplement existing fleet submarines and build up nuclear submarine numbers at a time when the United Kingdom only had a few. The Swiftsure class was a follow-on from the successful Valiant Class attack submarine. However, a number of improvements were incorporated into the new design including a cylindrical hull and improved sonar and torpedo systems. As a result of these improvements, the Swiftsure class was a marked step forward, as they were quieter, faster and could dive to greater depths than any previous British SSN, but they are now lagging far behind in terms of technology and capability. As with all attack submarines, the principle role of these "hunter-killer" vessels is to attack ships and other submarines. In this capacity they could support and protect a convoy or task-force. Additionally fleet submarines can be used in a surveillance role. The Swiftsure was a surprise choice to be the first British submarine to be fitted with the ability to fire the Tomahawk cruise missile, and has thus acquired a land attack role as well. The Swiftsure class is approaching the end of its operational life, having had a varied and active service, but is due to be replaced by the new Astute class SSN when it enters service in 2006.

SPECIFICATIONS

Builder:	Vickers Shipbuilding
Class:	Swiftsure
Number:	S-108
Mission:	attack submarine
Length:	82.9m (273ft)
Beam:	9.8m (32ft)
Displacement:	5000 tonnes (5080 tons)
Speed:	30 knots
Operating Depth:	230m (760ft)
Maximum Depth:	300m (990ft)
Crew:	116
Nuclear Weapons:	none
Conventional Weapons:	533mm (21in) torpedo, Harpoon
Sonar:	Marconi 2074 sonar suite
Navigation:	Kelvin Hughes Type 1006
Powerplant:	nuclear reactor, 15,000 shp
Date Commissioned:	1974

HMS SPLENDID

The Royal Navy Swiftsure class attack submarine HMS *Splendid* has been one of the most active vessels in the United Kingdom's submarine fleet over the last 20 years. She joined the fleet in 1981, and saw immediate action when the Argentine military junta invaded the Falkland Islands in 1982. She was part of the Task Force that set sail to reconquer the islands, and was one of four submarines that took part in the conflict. Though the submarine HMS *Conqueror* grabbed the headlines by sinking the Argentine cruiser *General Belgrano*, the presence of the four submarines persuaded the Argentine Navy to stay out of the war. After being retro-fitted in 1998, HMS *Splendid* became the first Royal Navy submarine capable of firing Tomahawk cruise missiles. She demonstrated this new ability when she destroyed a small building in the United States, 640km (400 miles) inland. When the strikes against Serbia began in March 1999 during the Kosovo crisis, HMS *Splendid* joined US warships in launching missiles at Serb targets, becoming the first British nuclear submarine to fire in anger since HMS *Conqueror* in 1982, reportedly destroying a radar site at Pristina airport. Though in the grand scheme of things this was more a gesture than of any great military importance, it signified a step forward in the Royal Navy's fighting capabilities.

SPECIFICATIONS

Builder:	*Vickers Shipbuilding*
Class:	*Swiftsure*
Number:	*S-112*
Mission:	*attack submarine*
Length:	*82.9m (273ft)*
Beam:	*9.8m (32ft)*
Displacement:	*5000 tonnes (5080 tons)*
Speed:	*30 knots*
Operating Depth:	*230m (760ft)*
Maximum Depth:	*300m (990ft)*
Crew:	*116*
Nuclear Weapons:	*none*
Conventional Weapons:	*533mm (21in) torpedo, TLAM*
Sonar:	*Marconi 2074 sonar suite*
Navigation:	*Kelvin Hughes Type 1006*
Powerplant:	*nuclear reactor, 15,000 shp*
Date Commissioned:	*1981*

HMS TRAFALGAR

The Trafalgar class attack submarine was the United Kingdom's primary anti-submarine and anti-shipping vessel during the latter years of the Cold War and into the 1990s. It was originally designed for Cold War operations in the Mediterranean and North Atlantic theatres, but has seen service in other parts of the world. The design is a follow-on from the successful Swiftsure class attack submarine but incorporated many improvements, making the class both faster and quieter than any previous British nuclear submarine. The principle role of these hunter-killer vessels, as they are colloquially known in the British submarine service, is to attack ships and other submarines that might otherwise endanger a convoy or task force. To achieve this aim the Trafalgar class is fitted with five 533mm (21in) torpedo tubes, which can fire either the Spearfish or Tigerfish torpedoes, launch the Sub Harpoon missile or deploy mines. Two of the class, HMS *Triumph* and HMS *Trafalgar*, have been retro-fitted to fire Tomahawk cruise missiles. It is expected that the remaining five boats of the class will all be able to launch the Tomahawk missile by 2006. The Trafalgar class has recently been under the media spotlight for a series of faults and cracks that forced all seven boats to be grounded for a short while. Despite this setback, the Trafalgar class submarine is still a most capable vessel.

SPECIFICATIONS

Builder:	Vickers Shipbuilding
Class:	Trafalgar
Number:	S-107
Mission:	attack submarine
Length:	85.3m (281ft)
Beam:	9.8m (32ft)
Displacement:	5200 tonnes (5283 tons)
Speed:	30 knots
Operating Depth:	300m (990ft)
Maximum Depth:	400m (1320ft)
Crew:	130
Nuclear Weapons:	none
Conventional Weapons:	533mm (21in) torpedo, TLAM
Sonar:	BAe Type 2007 sonar suite
Navigation:	Kelvin Hughes Type 1007
Powerplant:	nuclear reactor, 15,000 shp
Date Commissioned:	1983

HMS TRIUMPH

HMS *Triumph* is the last in a batch of seven Trafalgar class attack submarines to enter service with the British Royal Navy. Aside from the traditional "hunter-killer" role of the Trafalgar class, these boats are able to conduct intelligence-gathering operations and perform a surveillance role. These operations might involve moving close to enemy forces at sea, and monitoring their operations and movements whilst remaining undetected. This type of surveillance may also include underwater photography, sometimes of surface vessels. Similarly, the surveillance role may include the monitoring of a stretch of coastline using sophisticated video technology or digital photography. A submarine could stealthily approach a coastline in shallow water and assess the situation prior to an amphibious invasion or land action. To achieve this, all Trafalgar class boats are fitted with camera equipment and thermal-imaging scopes in their periscope arrays. The ability of an SSN to remain on active duty, totally indepedent from the need for support vessels and with flexible mission tasks, makes them useful in modern warfare. This independence was illustrated by HMS *Triumph* when she sailed to Australia in 1993 travelling 65,600km (41,000) miles submerged without any forward support. This remains the longest ever solo deployment by a nuclear submarine.

SPECIFICATIONS

Builder:	*Vickers Shipbuilding*
Class:	*Trafalgar*
Number:	*S-93*
Mission:	*attack submarine*
Length:	*85.3m (281ft)*
Beam:	*9.8m (32ft)*
Displacement:	*5200 tonnes (5283 tons)*
Speed:	*30+ knots*
Operating Depth:	*300m (990ft)*
Maximum Depth:	*400m (1320ft)*
Crew:	*130*
Nuclear Weapons:	*none*
Conventional Weapons:	*533mm (21in) torpedo, TLAM*
Sonar:	*BAe Type 2007 sonar suite*
Navigation:	*Kelvin Hughes Type 1007*
Powerplant:	*nuclear reactor, 15,000 shp*
Date Commissioned:	*1991*

HMS VANGUARD

The new Vanguard Class SSBN (Ship Submersible Ballistic Nuclear) provides the United Kingdom's only strategic and sub-strategic nuclear deterrent. The first Vanguard class submarine was launched in 1993 and was the replacement for the ageing Polaris SSBNs of the Resolution class. This class of submarines is extremely capable and provides the United Kingdom with a wide range of capabilities far beyond that of simple strategic deterrence. In its role of SSBN, the Vanguard has the capacity to carry 16 D-5 Trident II missiles, each with up to 12 independently targetable nuclear warheads. One Vanguard class boat can carry up to 192 individual warheads, though in reality it carries a maximum of 96, which has been recently reduced to 48. The Trident II missile has a range of up to 11,000km (6875 miles), and each warhead can hit its target with an accuracy of within 120m (360ft). In addition to its capability to launch nuclear missiles, the Vanguard class has been recently configured to launch the Tomahawk cruise missile (TLAM), which gives the vessel greater flexibility and capability. Each vessel of this class has four 533mm (21in) tubes, carrying the Tigerfish and Spearfish torpedoes. The Tigerfish Mark 24 Mod 2 torpedo is a wire-guided torpedo with a 134kg (295lb) warhead and the Spearfish is a wire-guided torpedo with a range of 65km (40 miles).

SPECIFICATIONS

Builder:	Vickers Shipbuilding
Class:	Vanguard
Number:	S-28
Mission:	ballistic missile submarine
Length:	149.3m (493ft)
Beam:	12.8m (42ft)
Displacement:	16,000 tonnes (16,256 tons)
Speed:	25 knots
Operating Depth:	300m (990ft)
Maximum Depth:	450m (1485ft)
Crew:	132
Nuclear Weapons:	16 x Trident II D-5 SLBMs
Conventional Weapons:	533mm (21in) torpedo, TLAM
Sonar:	BAE 2054 composite sonar system
Navigation:	Type 1007 I-band radar
Powerplant:	nuclear reactor, 27,500 shp
Date Commissioned:	1994

HMS VICTORIOUS

HMS *Victorious* is another one of the Royal Navy's four Vanguard class SSBNs, and was commissioned into service in 1995. In the face of decreasing defence budgets and changing geopolitical climates, the Vanguard class has been able to adapt itself from a purely strategic role, to something altogether more flexible, and thus ultimately more worthy of its phenomenal cost. The Vanguard class can now launch the Tomahawk cruise missile, which is able to strike at inland targets at ranges of over 1300km (400 miles) with great accuracy. This means that the Vanguard class can deploy covertly to any troublespot in the world, and sit off the coast collecting intelligence, able to strike at any moment should the order be given. The extremely powerful intelligence gathering capabilities of the Vanguard class, along with its state-of-the-art communications arrays, is also one of its most useful assets. During the conflict in the Balkans throughout the 1990s, and in the more recent Kosovo crisis, all communications traffic for the entire NATO alliance was sent through a Vanguard class submarine hiding in the Adriatic. Some have questioned the continuing utility of a strategic nuclear deterrent, but the Vanguard has shown itself able to cope with the rigours of the post-Cold War world, and able to find a place for its capabilities within the United Kingdom's force structure.

SPECIFICATIONS

Builder:	Vickers Shipbuilding
Class:	Vanguard
Number:	S-29
Mission:	ballistic missile submarine
Length:	149.3m (493ft)
Beam:	12.8m (42ft)
Displacement:	16,000 tonnes (16,293 tons)
Speed:	25 knots
Operating Depth:	300m (990ft)
Maximum Depth:	450m (1485ft)
Crew:	132
Nuclear Weapons:	16 x Trident II D-5 SLBMs
Conventional Weapons:	533mm (21in) torpedo, TLAM
Sonar:	BAE 2054 composite sonar system
Navigation:	Type 1007 I-band radar
Powerplant:	nuclear reactor, 27,500 shp
Date Commissioned:	1995

ASDS

Submarines have long been used for special operations carrying commandos, reconnaissance teams and agents on high-risk missions. Most special operations in US submarines are carried out by SEALs, the Sea-Air-Land teams trained for missions behind enemy lines. These special forces can be inserted by fixed-wing aircraft, helicopter, parachute or surface craft, but in most scenarios only submarines guarantee covert delivery. Once in the objective area, SEALs can carry out reconnaissance, monitoring enemy movements, and a host of other clandestine and often dangerous missions. Submarines are especially well suited for this role because of their high speed, endurance and stealth. The Advanced SEAL Delivery System (ASDS) is a long-range miniature submersible capable of delivering special forces for covert missions. ASDS provides improved range, speed and payload, and habitability for the crew and a SEAL squad. ASDS will be carried to its operational area by a host ship, currently a specially configured Los Angeles class, and in the future a Seawolf or Virginia class submarine. ASDS will also be air transportable by either C-5 or C-17 aircraft. A total of six ASDS will be built for the US Special Operations Command (USSOCOM), and will be able to perform a variety of tasks including covert insertion, reconnaissance and rescue.

SPECIFICATIONS

Builder:	Northrup Grumman
Class:	ASDS
Number:	n/a
Mission:	SEAL delivery submarine
Length:	19.8m (64ft)
Beam:	2.4m (8ft)
Displacement:	60 tonnes (59 tons)
Speed:	8 knots
Operating Depth:	unknown
Maximum Depth:	unknown
Crew:	2 + 8 SEALs
Nuclear Weapons:	none
Conventional Weapons:	none
Sonar:	classified
Navigation:	classified
Powerplant:	electric motor, 67 shp
Date Commissioned:	2001

EX-USS TROUT

The last operational diesel-electric submarine in the US Navy has been designated and modified for use as an operational underwater sonar target for anti-submarine warfare (ASW) exercises. The vessel will be operated by Naval Air Warfare Center Aircraft Division (NAWCAD) Detachment Key West. In addition to ASW training, the boat is used for testing and trials of new technologies. It is manned by a small crew while surfaced for transit, but unmanned while submerged. The boat is not assigned an official designation or name. Formerly USS *Trout*, it was decommissioned and stricken on 19 December 1978 and nominally transferred to Iran when relations between the two countries were buoyant. However, the vessel was never delivered following the Iranian revolution and she was laid up at Philadelphia while her ownership and fate were worked out. In 1994 she was sold back to the US Navy at scrap value. A vital training tool for the newest generation of anti-submarine units, the ex-USS *Trout* allows the US Navy to train its airborne naval anti-submarine units, such as the SH-60B Seahawk helicopter crews, to the highest level. It also gives them practical experience of hunting an actual submarine that has similar capabilities to other potential enemy vessels around the world, such as those used by China, North Korea and other Middle East states.

SPECIFICATIONS

Builder:	*Electric Boat*
Class:	*SSN-563 Tang (Modified)*
Number:	*SSN-566*
Mission:	*ASW training submarine*
Length:	*84.7m (278ft)*
Beam:	*8.2m (27ft)*
Displacement:	*2700 tonnes (2743 tons)*
Speed:	*16 knots*
Operating Depth:	*unknown*
Maximum Depth:	*unknown*
Crew:	*0 + 10*
Nuclear Weapons:	*none*
Conventional Weapons:	*none*
Sonar:	*unknown*
Navigation:	*unknown*
Powerplant:	*diesel-electric, 5600 shp*
Date Commissioned:	*1951 (re-introduced 1994)*

NR-1

NR-1, the first deep submergence vessel using nuclear power, was launched on 25 January 1969, and successfully completed her initial sea trials on 19 August 1969. It manoeuvres by four ducted thrusters, two in the front and two in the rear. The vehicle also has planes mounted on the sail, and a conventional rudder. NR-1's official missions have included search, object recovery, geological survey, oceanographic research, and installation and maintenance of underwater equipment. It was also in action following the loss of the Space Shuttle Challenger in 1986, searching for, identifying, and recovering critical parts of the Challenger craft. Militarily the NR-1 can be used for a number of covert operations in very deep water. It is doubtful that special forces would be deployed via the NR-1, but the vessel could be used for reconnaissance, for the emplacement of seabed acoustic devices and even the covert emplacement of mines in heavily defended areas. Though the NR-1 is not officially a military asset and has been used in a large number of civilian environments, such as archaeological studies, the vessel is certainly used for covert operations. The title "research vessel" is an often-used military euphemism for vessels used in clandestine missions, and the NR-1 is no exception. Despite its relative age, it is still a useful tool.

SPECIFICATIONS

Builder:	Electric Boat
Class:	NR-1
Number:	NR-1
Mission:	research/special operations
Length:	41.5m (136ft)
Beam:	3.6m (12ft)
Displacement:	394 tonnes (387 tons)
Speed:	5 knots
Operating Depth:	n/a
Maximum Depth:	1000m (3300ft)
Crew:	13
Nuclear Weapons:	none
Conventional Weapons:	none
Sonar:	Nautronics ATS
Navigation:	Benthos TR6000
Powerplant:	nuclear reactor
Date Commissioned:	1969

USS CHEYENNE

The USS *Cheyenne* is the United States Navy's most modern Los Angeles class attack submarine. It is 20 years younger than the original Los Angeles class boat, and thus it has incorporated some of military technology's more recent innovations into the same basic design. Though sharing many of the external appearances of the original Los Angeles class vessels, internally the newest boats are almost a different class given the vast improvements in computer technology during the 20 years that the Los Angeles class has been in production. The final 23 hulls (SSN-751 and later), referred to as 688I, are quieter, incorporate an advanced BSY-1 sonar suite combat system and have the ability to lay mines from their torpedo tubes. The weapons systems onboard a Los Angeles class submarine are truly awesome. The attack centre is the operational heart of the ship, and from where all offensive and defensive orders are made. The integrated fire-control computer is able to detect and classify targets and prepare a firing solution extremely quickly. The Mk48 torpedo that is used against other submarines or surface vessels is capable of travelling up to 55 knots and hitting a target over 8km (5 miles) away. Additionally, the Improved Los Angeles class has been configured for under-ice operations with the inclusion of a strengthened sail and bow planes moved from the sail.

SPECIFICATIONS

Builder:	*Newport News*
Class:	*SSN-688 Improved Los Angeles*
Number:	*SSN-773*
Mission:	*attack submarine*
Length:	*109.7m (360ft)*
Beam:	*10m (33ft)*
Displacement:	*6210 tonnes (6845 tons)*
Speed:	*32 knots*
Operating Depth:	*300m (950ft)*
Maximum Depth:	*400m (1320ft)*
Crew:	*129*
Nuclear Weapons:	*none*
Conventional Weapons:	*533mm (21in) torpedo, TLAM*
Sonar:	*BSY-1 sonar suite*
Navigation:	*AN/BPS-15 navigation radar*
Powerplant:	*nuclear reactor, 35,000 shp*
Date Commissioned:	*1996*

USS CHICAGO

The USS *Chicago*, though 10 years younger than her sister ship USS *Los Angeles*, is an almost identical vessel. Both boats use the same technology for fire control, navigation, sonar and propulsion. The S6G nuclear reactor on the Los Angeles class is a modified version of the D2G reactor first used on the CGN-25 Bainbridge class of guided missile cruiser. The nuclear powerplant gives these boats the ability to remain deployed and submerged for long periods of time, up to months at a time. Whilst the machinery is able to operate at sea for such long periods, the crew certainly could not without sophisticated life-support systems. Thus, the ships are outfitted with auxiliary equipment to provide for the needs of the crew. Atmosphere-control equipment replenishes oxygen used by the crew, and removes CO_2 and other atmospheric contaminants. The ship is equipped with two distilling plants, able to convert thousands of gallons of salt water into fresh water for drinking, washing and the propulsion plant. Sustained operation of the complex equipment and machinery on the ship requires the support of repair parts carried on board. The ship carries enough food to feed the crew for as long as 90 days. The logistical effort needed to keep a Los Angeles class attack submarine in fully operational order is a massive task requiring the expertise of many sailors.

SPECIFICATIONS

Builder:	*Newport News*
Class:	*SSN-688 Los Angeles*
Number:	*SSN-721*
Mission:	*attack submarine*
Length:	*109.7m (360ft)*
Beam:	*10m (33ft)*
Displacement:	*6210 tonnes (6845 tons)*
Speed:	*32 knots*
Operating Depth:	*300m (950ft)*
Maximum Depth:	*450m (1475ft)*
Crew:	*129*
Nuclear Weapons:	*none*
Conventional Weapons:	*533mm (21in) torpedo, TLAM*
Sonar:	*AN/BQQ-5D sonar array*
Navigation:	*AN/BPS-15 navigation radar*
Powerplant:	*nuclear reactor, 35,000 shp*
Date Commissioned:	*1986*

USS CONNECTICUT

The USS *Connecticut* is the second boat in the Seawolf series, and to all intents and purposes is identical to the USS *Seawolf*. Whilst the Seawolf class of submarine is a technological masterpiece in many respects, it was designed simply to counter the threat posed by Soviet submarines. However, the fall of the Soviet Union robbed the Seawolf class of its intended prey, and thus in the changed geopolitical climate, and given the shift in the manner in which wars are fought, USS *Connecticut* is searching for a role. The massive costs of the Seawolf programme made the submarine, at $3.5 billion US, prohibitively expensive and the number of submarines was limited to just three. However, all was not lost because much of the research effort that went into Seawolf has been used to good effect in the design of Seawolf's cheaper successor, the Virginia class SSN. Nonetheless, the USS *Connecticut* is a formidable machine, capable of taking on targets both on land, on the sea and under the waves more or less simultaneously. The Seawolf class can carry more armaments in a more varied package than any previous US SSN. It can hold 50 Tomahawk missiles, or 50 Sub Harpoon missiles, or 50 Mk48 torpedoes, or up to 100 mines. The mixture of armaments would be dependent on the mission, but a combination of all four types would be carried.

SPECIFICATIONS

Builder:	General Dynamics Electric Boat
Class:	SSN-21 Seawolf
Number:	SSN-22
Mission:	attack submarine
Length:	107.6m (353 ft)
Beam:	12.2m (40 feet)
Displacement:	9137 tonnes (9283 tons)
Speed:	35 knots
Operating Depth:	400m (1320ft)
Maximum Depth:	classified
Crew:	133
Nuclear Weapons:	none
Conventional Weapons:	660mm (30in) torpedo, TLAM
Sonar:	BSY-2 sonar/combat suite
Navigation:	BPS-16 navigation radar
Powerplant:	nuclear reactor, 52,000 shp
Date Commissioned:	1998

USS JIMMY CARTER

The USS *Jimmy Carter* is the third and final boat in the Seawolf class of submarines. However, Department of Defense chiefs have used the cancellation of the Seawolf series as an opportunity to use the advanced technology of the Seawolf in a novel and modified way, and the USS *Jimmy Carter* is the boat they have selected to experiment with. This said, the USS *Jimmy Carter* will be fully operational, but will utilize new technologies and techniques to explore the potential future of submarine warfare now that the traditional Soviet threat has diminished and the nature of modern conflict appears to require a different doctrine for submarines. To this end the USS *Jimmy Carter* has been comprehensively modified. The planned alterations include lengthening the hull section behind the sail and inserting an Ocean Interface section that will support a new Multi-Mission Project by opening larger payload apertures to the sea. It will also be able to support future concepts of offensive and defensive mine warfare in her ability to launch and recover a wide range of tethered and autonomous vehicles and sensors of varying sizes and shapes. In addition to these robust capabilities, USS *Jimmy Carter* will also be capable of supporting special operations forces with provision for operating the Dry Deck Shelter (DDS) and Advanced SEAL Delivery System (ASDS).

SPECIFICATIONS

Builder:	Electric Boat
Class:	SSN-21 Seawolf
Number:	SSN-23
Mission:	special operations submarine
Length:	107.6m (353 ft)
Beam:	12.2m (40 feet)
Displacement:	9137 tonnes (9283 tons)
Speed:	35 knots
Operating Depth:	400m (1325ft)
Maximum Depth:	classified
Crew:	133 + 50 special forces
Nuclear Weapons:	none
Conventional Weapons:	660mm (30in) torpedo, TLAM
Sonar:	BSY-2 sonar / combat suite
Navigation:	BPS-16 navigation radar
Powerplant:	nuclear reactor, 52,000 shp
Date Commissioned:	2001

USS KAMEHAMEHA

Originally commissioned as ballistic missile submarines, two remaining members of the Benjamin Franklin class of submarine were converted to special operations attack submarines, with a capacity for carrying and delivering special operations forces. They are equipped to covertly insert special operations forces into hostile territory. Like all submarines, they can sit off a coast for as long as needed, undetected, waiting to act or leave without raising tensions in the meantime. The boomers converted to dual Dry Dock Shelter (DDS) carriers are huge compared to the Sturgeon SSNs previously used for this role. On the SSBN the SEALs and crew can be berthed in greater comfort. Enough exercise equipment can be loaded for the SEALs and crew to maintain the physical conditioning required for mission success. SEAL mission planning, briefings and operations can be conducted with minimum crew disruption, whilst the crew are free to operate as if the SEALs were not on board. In August 1993, USS *Kamehameha* arrived in Pearl Harbor to become part of Submarine Squadron One. This vessel now regularly deploys in support of special warfare objectives throughout the Pacific and beyond. The USS *Kamehameha* is a very capable attack and special operations submarine, but is approaching the end of its service life.

SPECIFICATIONS

Builder:	Electric Boat
Class:	Modified Benjamin Franklin
Number:	SSN-642
Mission:	attack/SEAL delivery submarine
Length:	129m (425ft)
Beam:	10m (33ft)
Displacement:	8120 tonnes (8250 tons)
Speed:	25 knots
Operating Depth:	300m (990ft)
Maximum Depth:	400m (1320ft)
Crew:	135 + 65 SEALs
Nuclear Weapons:	none
Conventional Weapons:	533mm (21in) torpedo
Sonar:	IBM BQQ 6
Navigation:	BPS 15A
Powerplant:	nuclear reactor, 15,000 shp
Date Commissioned:	1965 (relaunched 1993)

USS L. MENDEL RIVERS

The USS *L. Mendel Rivers* is a modified Sturgeon class SSN submarines that carries a Dry Dock Shelter (DDS) aft of its conning tower. The DDS is used to launch SEAL teams from the safety of submersion into enemy waters without detection. This method of SEAL delivery is remarkably effective and has been used in many conflicts around the world. The SEAL team's mission is often some form of intelligence gathering or covert infiltration prior to a more conventional attack. The United States Navy SEALs are amongst the best-trained and equipped special forces units in the world. Aboard a submarine, they live in cramped conditions preparing themselves for the mission ahead. They can deploy themselves in a manner of ways. They can use scuba equipment to swim to shore, an inflatable dingy or even a small submarine. Once ashore, the submarine moves to a safer location than the drop-off point and loiters, monitoring communications and relaying information. When the SEAL team has completed its mission, the submarine returns stealthily to a pre-arranged area where it can once more covertly collect the troops into the DDS. If everything goes to plan, the enemy would never be aware that its defences had been penetrated and that a US submarine and special operations team had been involved.

SPECIFICATIONS

Builder:	Newport News
Class:	SSN-637 Sturgeon
Number:	SSN-686
Mission:	attack/SEAL delivery submarine
Length:	92m (302ft)
Beam:	9.7m (32ft)
Displacement:	5039 tonnes (5119 tons)
Speed:	25 knots
Operating Depth:	350m (1200ft)
Maximum Depth:	600m (1980ft)
Crew:	107 + SEAL teams
Nuclear Weapons:	none
Conventional Weapons:	533mm (21in) torpedo, Harpoon
Sonar:	BQS-13 active sonar
Navigation:	BPS-14/15 radar
Powerplant:	nuclear reactor, 15,000 shp
Date Commissioned:	1975

USS LOS ANGELES

The Los Angeles class SSN was designed almost exclusively for carrier battlegroup escort; they were fast, quiet, and could launch Mk48 and ADCAP torpedoes, Harpoon Anti-Ship Missiles, and land-attack Tomahawk cruise missiles. Cutting edge when they were launched, the new submarines were another major improvement in noise-reduction technology and speed. Escort duties include conducting anti-submarine warfare sweeping hundreds of miles ahead of the carrier battlegroup and conducting attacks against enemy vessels. Submarines of the Los Angeles class are still among the most advanced undersea vessels of their type in the world. While anti-submarine warfare is still their primary mission, and given their original remit as a Cold War weapon, the inherent characteristics of the submarine's stealth, mobility and endurance are still more than qualified to meet the challenges of the twenty-first century's turbulent global geopolitical climate. The Los Angeles class are able to get on station quickly, stay for an extended period of time and carry out a variety of missions including the deployment of special forces, minelaying and precision strike land attack, all of which are important concepts of military operation in the new millenium. These boats are well equipped to accomplish these tasks, even though the design is from a past era.

SPECIFICATIONS

Builder:	Newport News
Class:	SSN-688 Los Angeles
Number:	SSN-688
Mission:	attack submarine
Length:	109.7m (360ft)
Beam:	10m (33ft)
Displacement:	6210 tonnes (6845 tons)
Speed:	32 knots
Operating Depth:	300m (990ft)
Maximum Depth:	400m (1320ft)
Crew:	129
Nuclear Weapons:	none
Conventional Weapons:	533mm (21in) torpedo, TLAM
Sonar:	BSY-1 sonar suite
Navigation:	AN/BPS-15 navigation radar
Powerplant:	nuclear reactor, 35,000 shp
Date Commissioned:	1976

USS LOUISIANA

The last Ohio class SSBN to be rolled out by the United States Navy is the USS *Louisiana*. In light of the changing nature of the global political situation and the end of the Cold War, the United States Government decided that the SSBN programme should be limited to 18 boats. SSBNs form a key part of the TRIAD strategic deterrence for the US, with land-based and air-launched nuclear weapons. The Ohio class of SSBNs are equipped with two different types of missiles, depending largely on the age of the boat. The USS *Louisiana* is fitted with one of the most sophisticated nuclear missiles systems in the world, the D-5 Trident II. The D-5 is essentially an evolution of its predecessor the C-4 Trident I, as carried by the older Ohio class submarines. Carrying its compliment of MIRVs in its nose cone, the D-5 can deliver them onto different targets up to 7360km (4600 miles) away. Able to carry 24 missiles, each with six to eight 500-kiloton MIRVs, one Ohio class SSBN in the Atlantic could destroy every European capital city, every state capital in the United States and still have warheads to spare. This awesome quantity of firepower is second to none in the modern world. There is more to the Ohio class than pure firepower, however, as it is also equipped with some of the most sensitive and effective sensors and communications equipment in the world.

SPECIFICATIONS

Builder:	*Electric Boat*
Class:	*SSBN-726 Ohio*
Number:	*SSBN-743*
Mission:	*ballistic missile submarine*
Length:	*170.7m (560ft)*
Beam:	*12.7m (42ft)*
Displacement:	*19,000 tonnes (18,750 tons)*
Speed:	*25 knots*
Operating Depth:	*300m (990ft)*
Maximum Depth:	*450m (1485ft)*
Crew:	*155*
Nuclear Weapons:	*24 x D-5 Trident II*
Conventional Weapons:	*533mm (21in) torpedo*
Sonar:	*BQS-13 active sonar*
Navigation:	*Raytheon navigation sonar*
Powerplant:	*nuclear reactor, 60,000 shp*
Date Commissioned:	*1997*

USS OHIO

The USS *Ohio* is the first ship in the Ohio class of fleet ballistic missile (FBM) submarines. This class replaced the ageing FBM submarines from the 1960s, and was brought into service during the early 1980s. The Ohio class submarine is vastly more capable than its predecessors, and is one of the most advanced pieces of technology on the planet. SSBN-726 class FBM submarines can carry 24 ballistic missiles each with 7 MIRV warheads that can be accurately delivered to selected targets from almost anywhere in the world's oceans. The hull has been designed to allow for greater speed whilst submerged, but also retaining an unprecedented level of stealth, making detection much harder. The larger hull of the Ohio class can accommodate more weapons of larger size and greater range, as well as sophisticated computerized electronic equipment for improved weapon guidance and sonar performance. The Ohio class submarines are specifically designed to be able to operate at sea for exceptionally long periods of time. To reduce the time needed in port for replenishment, and also to make such processes easier, three large logistics hatches are fitted to provide large-diameter resupply and repair openings. These hatches allow the rapid transfer of supply pallets, equipment replacement modules and machinery.

SPECIFICATIONS

Builder:	*Electric Boat*
Class:	*SSBN-726 Ohio*
Number:	*SSBN-726*
Mission:	*ballistic missile submarine*
Length:	*170.7m (560ft)*
Beam:	*12.7m (42ft)*
Displacement:	*19,000 tonnes (18,750 tons)*
Speed:	*25 knots*
Operating Depth:	*300m (990ft)*
Maximum Depth:	*450m (1485ft)*
Crew:	*155*
Nuclear Weapons:	*24 x C-4 Trident I*
Conventional Weapons:	*533mm (21in) torpedo*
Sonar:	*BQQ-6 passive sonar*
Navigation:	*Raytheon navigation sonar*
Powerplant:	*nuclear reactor, 60,000 shp*
Date Commissioned:	*1981*

USS PARCHE

Sturgeon class submarines were built for anti-submarine warfare in the late 1960s and 1970s. Using the same propulsion system as the predecessor SSN-585 Skipjack and SSN-594 Permit classes, the larger Sturgeons sacrificed speed for greater combat capabilities. They have been modified to carry the Harpoon missile, the Tomahawk cruise missile, as well as the Mk48 and ADCAP torpedoes. The torpedo tubes are located amidships to accommodate the bow-mounted sonar. The sail-mounted dive planes rotate to a vertical position for breaking through the ice when surfacing in Arctic regions. Beginning with SSN-678 Archerfish, units of this class had a longer hull, giving them more living and working space than previous submarines of the Sturgeon Class. A total of six Sturgeon class boats have been modified to carry the SEAL Dry Deck Shelter (DDS), one in 1982 and five between 1988 and 1991. In this configuration they are primarily tasked with the covert insertion of special forces troops from the attached DDS. The Dry Deck Shelter is a submersible launch hanger with a hyperbaric pressure chamber that attaches to the ship's weapon shipping hatch. Rapidly being phased out in favour of the Los Angeles and Seawolf class vessels, this venerable and flexible workhorse of the submarine attack fleet continues to operate to this day.

SPECIFICATIONS

Builder:	Ingalls Shipbuilding
Class:	SSN-637 Sturgeon
Number:	SSN-683
Mission:	attack/SEAL delivery submarine
Length:	92m (302ft)
Beam:	9.7m (32ft)
Displacement:	5039 tonnes (5119 tons)
Speed:	25 knots
Operating Depth:	300m (990ft)
Maximum Depth:	350m (1155ft)
Crew:	107
Nuclear Weapons:	none
Conventional Weapons:	533mm (21in) torpedo, TLAM
Sonar:	BQS-13 active sonar
Navigation:	BPS-14/15 radar
Powerplant:	nuclear reactor, 15,000 shp
Date Commissioned:	1974

USS SANTA FE

The USS *Santa Fe* is an improved version of the Los Angeles class submarine, and one of the most modern Los Angeles class boats in US Navy service. All the improved versions of the Los Angeles class SSN are equipped with the Tomahawk land attack (TLAM) cruise missile. The addition of this weapons system to the SSN is a vital step in the evolution of the attack submarine. Since the end of the Cold War, the Los Angeles class submarine has lost its primary enemy as the Russian threat has disappeared and its ballistic and attack submarines have all but fallen into disrepair. Finding another role for the billions of dollars of SSN capability has been one of the prime focuses in recent years. The addition of the Tomahawk cruise missile appears to have solved the problem. Whilst continuing to fulfil its role as protection for a carrier group, it can also take part in force projection and precision strike missions with the Tomahawk cruise missile. This modern submarine can sneak undetected silently into enemy waters, and launch a Tomahawk whilst still submerged at a target over 1200km (750 miles) into enemy territory. This ability to strike at a target with great accuracy whilst remaining hidden is a huge advantage in modern warfare. It is also a great assistance in the peace-enforcement or peacekeeping operations that the United States takes part in.

SPECIFICATIONS

Builder:	Electric Boat
Class:	SSN-688 Improved Los Angeles
Number:	SSN-763
Mission:	attack submarine
Length:	109.7m (360ft)
Beam:	10m (33ft)
Displacement:	6210 tonnes (6845 tons)
Speed:	32 knots
Operating Depth:	300m (990ft)
Maximum Depth:	400m (1320ft)
Crew:	129
Nuclear Weapons:	none
Conventional Weapons:	533mm (21in) torpedo, TLAM
Sonar:	BSY-1 sonar suite
Navigation:	AN/BPS-15 navigation radar
Powerplant:	nuclear reactor, 35,000 shp
Date Commissioned:	1993

USS SEAWOLF

The USS *Seawolf* is the first of a new class of submarines designed to operate autonomously against the world's most capable submarine and surface threats. The primary mission of the Seawolf would have been to destroy Soviet ballistic missile submarines before they could attack American targets, had the Cold War not ended in 1991. The Soviet submarines were and remain one of the most effective elements of their intercontinental ballistic missile arsenal, but they no longer present a genuine threat to US interests. In addition to their capabilities in countering enemy submarines and surface shipping, Seawolf submarines are suited for battlespace-preparation roles, and are thus useful in the post-Cold War era. Incorporation of sophisticated electronics gives the Seawolf enhanced indications and warning, surveillance and communications capabilities that are extremely useful in a battlegroup. These platforms are capable of integrating into a battlegroup's infrastructure, providing support and protection, or shifting rapidly into a land battle support role with its Tomahawk land-attack missiles (TLAM). Seawolf also incorporates the latest in quiet technology to keep pace with the threat then posed by an aggressive Soviet Union. It is said that the Seawolf class is quieter at its tactical speed of 25 knots than a Los Angeles class submarine at pierside.

SPECIFICATIONS

Builder:	*Electric Boat*
Class:	*SSN-21 Seawolf*
Number:	*SSN-21*
Mission:	*attack submarine*
Length:	*107.6m (353 ft)*
Beam:	*12.2m (40 feet)*
Displacement:	*9137 tonnes (9283 tons)*
Speed:	*35 knots*
Operating Depth:	*400m (1325ft)*
Maximum Depth:	*classified*
Crew:	*133*
Nuclear Weapons:	*none*
Conventional Weapons:	*660mm (30in) torpedo, TLAM*
Sonar:	*BSY-2 sonar suite*
Navigation:	*BPS-16 navigation radar*
Powerplant:	*nuclear reactor, 52,000 shp*
Date Commissioned:	*1997*

USS TENNESSEE

The USS *Tennessee* SSBN is an Ohio class submarine fitted with the D-5 Trident II nuclear weapon. As part of the United States TRIAD system of nuclear deterrence, the Ohio class submarine must be able to deliver its firepower onto its target within minutes of receiving a launch instruction. To this end the USS *Tennessee* must be within range of its target. Designed and built during the unstable days of the Cold War, the Ohio class submarines were designed to patrol the seas within range of the Soviet Union, able to launch at a moment's notice. All the while Soviet hunter submarines would be searching for them. The Soviet Akula class attack submarines were designed specifically to counter the threat of US ballistic missile submarines, and the two vessels played a game of cat-and-mouse under the Polar ice caps for much of the 1980s. Thus the Ohio was designed to be especially quiet. Even though it is some years old and technology has moved forward, the Ohio class is still one of the quietest submarines in the world. Much of the technology and design that makes it so stealthy is top secret to this day, and whilst the original enemy has disappeared, the Ohio class is still able to patrol hostile waters without detection, collecting intelligence and keeping America's interests abroad safe from hostile intent. USS *Tennessee* is expected to serve until 2020.

SPECIFICATIONS

Builder:	*Electric Boat*
Class:	*SSBN-726 Ohio*
Number:	*SSBN-734*
Mission:	*ballistic missile submarine*
Length:	*170.7m (560ft)*
Beam:	*12.7m (42ft)*
Displacement:	*19,000 tonnes (19,304 tons)*
Speed:	*25 knots*
Operating Depth:	*300m (990ft)*
Maximum Depth:	*450m (1485ft)*
Crew:	*155*
Nuclear Weapons:	*24 x D-5 Trident II*
Conventional Weapons:	*533mm (21in) torpedo*
Sonar:	*BQS-13 active sonar*
Navigation:	*Raytheon navigation sonar*
Powerplant:	*nuclear reactor, 60,000 shp*
Date Commissioned:	*1988*

USS TEXAS

The Virginia class submarines, of which the USS *Texas* will be one of the earliest examples, is arguably a quantum leap in submarine technology and doctrine. Taking much of its design and development directly from the halted Seawolf class submarine, the Virginia class will stand head and shoulders above any of its rivals across the globe. The most innovative feature of the Virginia class is undoubtedly the integral lock-in/lock-out chamber. This will be used for delivering special forces teams from the boat in much the same way as the Dry Dock Shelter (DDS) systems do. However, the difference is that the Virginia class submarines will host the new Advanced SEAL Delivery System (ASDS), a miniature submarine for covert use by special forces. The chamber will also give the Virginia class much greater flexibility and size in payload than the DDS system does. This evolution of the DDS system into an attack submarine highlights the US Navy's desire for greater operational flexibility and capability from its submarine force. Along with the traditional attack role and the new special warfare role, the Virginia class will also be able to attack land targets with their Tomahawk cruise missiles. The integration of all these different systems into one submarine marks a shift in US operational doctrine, and undoubtedly leads the way for future submarine development.

SPECIFICATIONS

Builder:	*Newport News*
Class:	*SSN-774 Virginia*
Number:	*SSN-775*
Mission:	*attack submarine*
Length:	*114m (377ft)*
Beam:	*10.3m (34ft)*
Displacement:	*7800 tonnes (7924 tons)*
Speed:	*28 knots*
Operating Depth:	*400m (1320ft)*
Maximum Depth:	*classified*
Crew:	*113*
Nuclear Weapons:	*none*
Conventional Weapons:	*533mm (21in) torpedo, TLAM*
Sonar:	*TB-29 towed array*
Navigation:	*BPS-16 navigation radar*
Powerplant:	*S9G nuclear reactor*
Date Commissioned:	*2005*

USS VIRGINIA

The USS *Virginia* is the first in the new class of attack submarine. It is an advanced stealth multi-mission nuclear-powered submarine for deep-ocean anti-submarine warfare and for littoral (shallow water) operations. Although the Seawolf submarine was developed to provide an eventual replacement for the US Navy Los Angeles class submarines in combating Soviet forces, the prohibitive unit cost and changing strategic requirements led to the US Navy defining a smaller new-generation attack submarine. The noise level of the Virginia is equal to that of the US Navy Seawolf, SSN 21, with a lower acoustic signature than the Russian Improved Akula class and the proposed Russian Fourth Generation Attack Submarines. To achieve this low acoustic signature, the Virginia incorporates newly designed anechoic coatings, isolated deck structures and a new design of propulsor. The submarine is equipped with 12 vertical missile-launch tubes and four 533mm (21in) torpedo tubes. The vertical launching system has the capacity to launch 16 Tomahawk submarine launched cruise missiles in a single salvo. There is capacity for up to 26 Mk48 ADCAP Mod 6 torpedoes, and Sub Harpoon anti-ship missiles can be fired from the torpedo tubes. Mk60 CAPTOR mines may also be fitted. The USS *Virginia* also carries the Advanced SEAL Delivery System (ASDS).

SPECIFICATIONS

Builder:	*Electric Boat*
Class:	*SSN-774 Virginia*
Number:	*SSN-774*
Mission:	*attack submarine*
Length:	*114m (377ft)*
Beam:	*10.3m (34ft)*
Displacement:	*7800 tonnes (7924 tons)*
Speed:	*28 knots*
Operating Depth:	*400m (1325ft)*
Maximum Depth:	*classified*
Crew:	*113*
Nuclear Weapons:	*none*
Conventional Weapons:	*533mm (21in) torpedo, TLAM*
Sonar:	*TB-29 Towed Array*
Navigation:	*BPS-16 navigation radar*
Powerplant:	*S9G nuclear reactor*
Date Commissioned:	*2004*

INDEX